Dr. David Brandt

Is That All There Is?

*Overcoming Disappointment in an
Age of Diminished Expectations*

POSEIDON PRESS

NEW YORK

Copyright © 1984 by David Brandt
All rights reserved
including the right of reproduction
in whole or in part in any form
A Poseidon Press Book
Published by Pocket Books, A Division of Simon & Schuster, Inc.
Simon & Schuster Building
Rockefeller Center
1230 Avenue of the Americas
New York, New York 10020
POSEIDON PRESS is a trademark of Simon & Schuster, Inc.
Designed by Eve Kirch
Manufactured in the United States of America

10 9 8 7 6 5 4 3 2 1

Library of Congress Cataloging in Publication Data
Brandt, David.
    Is that all there is?

    Bibliography: p.
    1. Disappointment. 2. Expectation (Psychology)
I. Title.
BF575.D57B73 1983   158'.1   83-19216
ISBN 0-671-45892-2

ACKNOWLEDGMENTS

Many people gave generously of their time and effort to the inspiration, conception, and refinement of this book. I want to thank: John White for his help with research; Lizbeth Hamlin for her insights during the early formulation; Richard Mullins for his contribution to the issue of narcissism; Bob Kriegel for his continual support and helpful feedback throughout.

Thanks as well to Martha Freebairn-Smith and Robert Brandt, patient and sensitive readers of the manuscript who gave thoughtful and incisive suggestions as well as encouragement and reassurance.

On the publication side, I am grateful to Sharon Cook for her help with editing and word processing and her tolerance of my essentially obsessive nature. My appreciation is also extended to my editor Ann Patty and her associate Pat Capon for their patience and expertise and to my agent Harvey Klinger, who made the whole thing possible.

I extend special acknowledgment to Jerry Polon, who gave more than any colleague could realistically be expected to give. His long and detailed labor over these pages was an act of exceptional generosity.

Further thanks to my life partner Laurie Brandt, who not only served as my live-in therapist but supplied most of the seminal thoughts on which this book is constructed. On this project as on every other, she gave of herself as only love would allow. For that particular quality of devotion and for her passionate mind, I am deeply grateful.

Finally, I want to thank the many friends, relatives and patients whose stories appear in one form or another in the text. It is your experience that gives immediacy and life to the book.

To Laurie:
Whose love transcends even
the barrier of nearness

Contents

Both the Trees and the Forest • Denise: A Disappointed Body • The Posture of Defeat • The Despairing Face • Breathing: Sigh without Relief

CHRONIC DISAPPOINTMENT STYLES

Introduction

This book is about the oldest of human experiences—the loss of dreams, the failure of expectations. All of recorded history and literature speak of this theme. Moses descending from Sinai, tablets in hand, profoundly disappointed and rageful as his people prostrated themselves before the golden calf. Napoleon, standing erect at Waterloo, watching his dreams die before British cannonfire. Madame Curie, on the brink of discovery in her laboratory, struggling against repeated failure to unleash the magical powers of radium.

The course of human events is strewn with the remnants of unfulfilled wishes, of outcomes never attained, seeds bearing no fruit. Disappointment is a universal theme. It encompasses the great and the small. We all hope and dream. Inevitably, we are disappointed. Our lives go on, perhaps a little less brightly.

For the past few years I have been interested in disappointment, not only from a professional point of view but from a personal standpoint as well. After twelve years as a successful psychologist in a long-standing and satisfying marriage, I found my life filled with chronic dissatisfaction and disappointment. Until then I had had these feelings only intermittently, isolated experiences which I took to be par for life's course. But now my feelings of disappointment seemed prolonged and deep. Every galaxy in my universe was tinged with the pallor of failed wishes. Initially, I thought this was an indication that I was suffering through an intense, but necessary, developmental passage. But as I observed myself, I began to see the issue in a new light.

To be sure, the developmental crisis was real. I suffered from a loss of illusion characteristic of the mid-thirties. My future was shrinking. My options were obviously more limited than when I was twenty-five. I couldn't be a concert pianist, running back for the 49ers, and budding young Freud, as I had once hoped. It was hard enough to give up two of these goals. What really disturbed me was the thought I might have to give up all three! At the same time I realized my disappointment was more than a midlife passage. The kind of person I was, the specific and enduring personality traits which characterized me, influenced the expectations I had for myself. I became aware that I had always felt a certain sense of privilege. For a number of reasons—all related to my family and my role in it—I had come to believe I was entitled to special treatment in the world. I was the exception to "No exceptions, please." Having such expectations guaranteed my disappointment. The rest of the world, unaware of the privilege it was obliged to grant me, responded as if I were just another mortal. My expectations were continually greater than my actual experience. The result? Disappointment of the first order.

I also began to realize that I was not alone in my disappointment. My patients were complaining about it as well, suffering through it without calling it by its proper name. They used the jargon of the day to describe their condition: alienation, depression, dysphoria. But much of what they reported was fundamentally the experience of disappointment: A, who was "depressed" by his sexual life, was actually disappointed by his wife's disinterest in sexual matters. B, who couldn't get along with her children, was disappointed by their performance in school. And so forth.

In a nation of huge material resource and economic opportunity, where the very pursuit of happiness is recognized in the founding declaration, could the degree of personal disappointment be on the rise? It certainly seemed so if complaints about relationships, family, sex, and work were to be taken seriously.

Undoubtedly, the failing economic fortunes of the country are a factor in this trend. Many dreams have already been shattered by plant closings, mortgage foreclosures, and bankruptcies. The Baby Boom Generation, that huge cohort of seventy million Americans born after World War Two and now just entering middle age, has been hardest hit. Raised in the halcyon days of the fifties with higher expectations and greater privilege than any group before it, these young people expected to settle into the easy success they had been promised. But the combination of intense competition, created by their large numbers, and the economic downswing have dashed those expectations and beaten down their hopes.

Yet the high material expectations of the Boom Generation and a failing marketplace do not altogether explain the issue.

Disappointment is a problem that transcends economics. As I stood in the checkout line of the local supermarket one day, another part of the puzzle fell into place. On the magazine racks in front of me, one boldfaced headline after another promised a better personal life through psychological intervention and attitude manipulation. If these mass-produced epistles were to be believed, one could learn how to love, succeed through coercion, and live out the wildest of fantasies simply by following the formulas contained in the text. It was only a matter of acquiring the proper technique. The pop-psychology revolution, which has put brief therapy on the radio and made "actualize" a household word, has brought with it the promise of individual fulfillment and personal satisfaction. But it has created an opposite effect as well. Assuring us of an easy, quick path to nirvana, it has given the false impression that personal change is a simple, painless matter. There is a part in each of us that deeply wants to believe this notion and falls prey to its ready appeal. The problem is that we have become addicted to the promise even though the remedy has been faulty. Shakespeare wrote:

> *I am giddy, expectation whirls me round.*
> *The imaginary relish is so sweet*
> *That it enchants my sense.*

But these fantasies of effortless personal transformation have, in fact, produced greater disappointment. The purveyors of quick psychological solutions have ironically enlarged the scope of the problem.

> *Hope tells a flattering tale,*
> *Delusive, vain and hollow.*
> *Ah! let not hope prevail,*
> *Lest disappointment follow.*

No era is without its disappointments, but today we suffer from an unparalleled case of inflated hopes and expectations. Disappointment flourishes in this sort of environment.

One purpose of this book is to serve as an initial antidote for those whose hopes exceed psychological reality. However, no promises are made. They would merely encourage the very situation we wish to avoid. Instead, I have in mind a larger purpose: to understand the psychology of disappointment, the nature and scope of the phenomenon. I want to unwrap the mysteries of this troublesome experience, show the variety of human responses to it, and reveal, surprisingly, how each of us can use disappointment to our own gain.

My personal struggles have led me to seek some sort of remedy that I can apply in a variety of circumstances involving disappointment, a "bromide" to be used to break the cycle of negative feeling associated with failed expectation. I have constructed such a method and have used it successfully to deal with isolated experiences of disappointment. I share it with the reader along with a word of caution. Repetitive patterns of disappointment are fundamentally related to enduring traits in our personalities. A remedial model can have only limited effect without recognition of the relationship between character and expectation. With this in mind I have emphasized three styles of disappointment in order to demonstrate how particular elements of the individual's character contribute to the kind and extent of experienced disappointment. You may well find your own story contained within one or more of these categories.

I have said disappointment is an inevitable consequence of human experience, and so it remains. My war with this chronic malaise is not over, but it has been reduced to a few infrequent infirmities. The degree to which it interferes with personal happiness can be diminished by knowledge of the disappointment process, the social forces that influence expectation, and the developmental and personality traits which may encourage it. With this information, disappointment becomes an ally, teaching us hard lessons about the limitations of reality and the need for adaptation and flexibility in a constantly changing universe. I hope this book will provide such knowledge.

David Brandt
Muir Beach, California

CHAPTER 1

The Best-Laid Plans

The best laid schemes
O' mice and men gang aft a-gley
An' le'e us nought
But grief an' pain for promis'd joy.
Robert Burns

You're sitting alone at a party. An attractive man approaches and begins a conversation. He has an appealing manner, and you find yourself immediately drawn to him. You like his quick wit and irreverence and are just about to tell him so when he gets up, mumbles an excuse, and leaves the room. You're surprised and feel a sense of loss.

You've started a second career after ten years in a profession you found unfulfilling. Retraining required three years of classwork. After some months on the job you discover that much of what you had expected from your second career was only a fantasy. The new work is no more satisfying than the old. You feel frustrated and confused.

You're working very hard on an important proposal for your boss, spending weekends and evenings to perfect your report. You're proud of your effort and submit the proposal with a sense of accomplishment. Your boss reads it a week after submission and writes a short memo that your work was acceptable. You feel resentful and cheated.

You're in bed with your spouse on vacation. This is the first quiet time you have had alone since you left home, although the days have been romantic and you've enjoyed each other. You make love, but the experience is familiar and dull, as if this were any other night. You feel a sense of desperation.

What do you make of these situations? Do they strike a sympathetic chord? Or are they merely the sort of unfortunate circumstances which happen to other people? Chances are, at least one of these experiences will sound familiar to you. If not, perhaps you are one of a small, fortunate, and privileged minority who has never been let down, never suffered from disappointment.

Disappointment is not the sort of subject we like to initiate at dinner parties. It might be appropriate in the therapist's office or at the Complainers' Ball, but not in general conversation. The word disappointment seems too trivial and minor-league to describe our real difficulties. We're all disappointed at some time or another. To depict ourselves as disappointment sufferers doesn't elicit much sympathy or understanding. "Big deal" is the usual response. It's a little like complaining about ingrown toenails. They hurt, but who cares?

Besides, we rarely think of ourselves as disappointed. We

prefer "dissatisfied" or "depressed," less specific feeling states that carry more psychological weight. But disappointed we are. Carrying the burden of unmet expectations on our backs, we are like the hikers whose rucksacks increase in weight as they traverse life's many trails. We'd like to get rid of that backpack, but how?

Few people have examined the patterns of disappointment in their lives. At best, they may have encountered the isolated experience, questioning why they should feel so cheated and dismayed and wondering about the power that disappointment holds over them. Still fewer have considered what disappointment really is. What are the ingredients of this bitter soup, sipped with the silver plastic as well as the spoon? We need to ask this important question if we want to relinquish the burden on our shoulders.

What Is Disappointment? The Thoughts and Feelings

Is disappointment merely dissatisfaction? Is it simply an experience of depression or loss? Disappointment certainly contains elements of each, but it is a distinct phenomenon, on the rise in our culture; a phenomenon of the eighties, surely, but one which has existed since the first porridge tasted like clay or the first fire went out. To put it in the simplest of terms, disappointment is unmet positive expectation. We expected X to happen. It did not. We are disappointed. It involves loss, of course, but not tangible loss, such as the death of a child or the theft of a valued possession. Disappointment is rather the loss of an anticipated idea.

People react differently to disappointment. Some feel anger, despair, defeat. Others do not allow themselves to feel much of anything but confusion. Generally, the most common initial reaction is a sense of shocked dispossession, as if we had lost something dear to us. It is similar to the winning home run miraculously stolen in the last inning by the glove of the opposition center fielder. We feel the loss of an outcome so strongly expected that we nearly assumed it had already happened. We could almost taste it, and therefore we feel cheated, as if, indeed, our team had already won the game. Having been so blatantly robbed, we are alarmed and disbelieving, and these feelings, in turn, are followed by anger, sadness, often self-pity, a sense of loss, and finally acceptance of the unsatisfactory outcome. The disappointment process is a six-stage cycle that follows a general pattern regardless of the content of the expectation or the intensity of the feeling. (For a more detailed discussion of this cycle, see Chapter Three.) Those who are unable to move through the cycle hold onto their discomfort and loss for prolonged periods. Eventually they become resentful and cynical and their world view is laced with misanthropy and pessimism. They become acutely aware of impossibility and focus on the limitations of existence. They appear to be chronically locked in disappointment.

Expectation: Where It All Begins

No one wishes disappointment on themselves. We tolerate it as inevitable because we cannot see a means to eliminate it. Alexander Pope wrote: "Blessed is the man who expects nothing for he shall never be disappointed." Was he suggesting that expectation can be eliminated from the human repertoire, thereby preventing disappointment? Is expectation the real problem? Expectation is simply the anticipation of an outcome, but we know it must be more than this by our crestfallen reaction when the outcome is not achieved. Positive expectation really has a dual nature: the belief that an event will occur and the desire for it to do so. Based on past experience, knowledge of the physical universe, or intuition, we anticipate possibility. We form a subjective evaluation of our prospects. And we believe with some certainty that we are correct. But our prognosis is also influenced by our wish for a specific outcome. We hope an event will happen. We look forward to it, and if it fails to occur, we feel bad. The lost idea we spoke about earlier is, in reality, a lost wish.

Examine the illustrations at the beginning of this chapter. Underlying each expectation you will find a wish. The woman at the party hopes her new acquaintance will stay. Perhaps she wishes to develop a relationship or run away to Acapulco with him; we can only speculate about the exact nature of her hopes. But when he leaves, her expectation is unsatisfied. She has been dispossessed of her wish, and she responds with surprise and a sense of loss. The hard-working employee expects a strong positive reaction to match his effort. He wishes for recognition and approval from his boss. When he receives minimal acknowledgment, he feels slighted.

It is the wish contained within every expectation that gives it life and energy. Without the wish an expectation would simply be a probability, a calculated belief about the future. Functioning in computerlike fashion, the mathematical mind might say, "Taking all factors into account, there is a fifteen percent chance that my husband, Fred, will want to make love this evening. With such a low probability I cannot anticipate this will occur." But because we are human we tend to process the same expectation in this manner: "It would be really nice to make love tonight. I know Fred might not be in the mood, but he'll come around." Thus the plan for the evening has been influenced by both probability and wish. The concession to probability is the consideration that Fred might not be in the mood, but the wish carries the day. "He'll come around." In a situation such as this, when a hoped-for outcome gets the better of a realistic assessment of possibility, disappointment is likely and psychological pain is the result.

Can we then be the blessed man or woman without expectation suggested by Alexander Pope? Unlikely. Eliminating expectation is similar to extinguishing curiosity or fantasy. Neither will go away no matter how we program the cognitive computer. The best we can hope for is a diminution. In Samuel Beckett's wonderfully paradoxical play, *Waiting for Godot*, we see the irrational and indefatigable quality of expectation stripped naked. Estragon and Vladimir are waiting for Godot on a bleak country road. He does not come, but sends a messenger in his stead who announces Godot will arrive the next day. The next day arrives. No Godot. Only a messenger with the same announcement. And so on. Yet Estragon and Vladimir persevere. They wait and wait in the face of accumulated time, hoping for Godot to show up. It is an allegory about life. Estragon remarks: "Nothing happens, nobody comes, nobody goes, it's awful!" Finally, after repeated expectation and disappointment:

Vladimir: We'll hang ourselves to-morrow. Unless Godot comes.

Estragon: And if he comes?
Vladimir: We'll be saved.

The implication is that only hope can save them. Without their wishes, there is no direction, no meaning, nothing. Godot will never come. His arrival is irrelevant. They, however, will continue to expect it.

Estragon: I can't go on like this.
Vladimir: That's what you think.

And their life will be given direction by their expectation:

Vladimir: What are we doing here, *that* is the question. And we are blessed in this, that we happen to have the answers. . . . Yes, in this immense confusion one thing alone is clear. We are waiting for Godot to come.

Is Beckett writing about the absurdity or the necessity of expectation and wish? The matter is left up to each reader. But it is apparent that the playwright is telling us that expectation and hope are part of the human condition.

The Benefits of Expectation

Expectation has a functional side to it as well. We organize our responses to the future with our expectations. We could not plan tomorrow's shopping, prepare for the predicted storm, put aside money for our daughter's education without anticipating the future. Expectation provides us with a sense of security. It allows us a rough knowledge of what may occur so we are not overwhelmed by events which, out of the blue, might destroy our composure.

The wish component in expectation also has a functional nature. Wishes are affirmations of the future. Lying in a hospital bed suffering pain and discomfort we may despair, but our wishes create for us the possibility that things will improve. They assume a future exists and give us hope. But they are motivators as well. It is often from our wishes that we derive the will to act and the strength to improve and heal ourselves. The inspired story of the dying patient whose unwavering wish for recovery motivates a "spontaneous remission" of symptoms is now part of contemporary folklore. Wishes are acknowledged as powerful medicine by both the shaman and the psychologist.

Imagine a life devoid of wishes. It would be rather bland and dull, like a rainbow of muted color or a stew without seasoning—acceptable but unexciting. Wishes are like the seedlings that miraculously break through the cracks in the concrete, persistently reaching for the sun. One way or another they will find expression, if not in conscious activity then through the mechanism of the unconscious mind. Freud demonstrated nearly seventy years ago that our wishes surface in dreams no matter how we may inhibit them in our daily life. We have only to examine fantasies, verbal errors, handwriting, material choices—even presidential doodles— to see the omnipresent quality of wishes.

The Problems of Investing in Expectation

Expectation is not evil in and of itself. Our problem really lies in how we relate to it—how important our expectations are to us and how willing we are to modify or surrender them. Those who suffer from chronic disappointment are the same individuals who overinvest in a particular outcome. Their expectations tend to rule them rather than the other way around. They are unwilling and seemingly unable to adapt to the unexpected. Caught in a web of their own making, they cannot see that they struggle against themselves. Most, in fact, will defend the need for their specific expectations as if they could not survive without them. Nothing could be more self-deceiving.

Why do people invest so dearly in expectation? Remember, no one really invests in the *belief* that an outcome will occur. What we invest in is the *wish* for that outcome. After all, if we anticipate we will like a movie and find it is a dud, why not give up the expectation and accept the reality as quickly as possible? The moviegoer who sits through the picture holding fast to a wish for excellence will leave disappointed. His friend who acknowledges the mediocrity of the film and relinquishes his wish will leave early or find some other amusement in the experience.

It is the wish within each expectation that hooks us and maintains our emotional investment. We don't relinquish our hopes easily. They are like small, precious stones held close to the chest as we walk through troubled neighborhoods. They are to be protected and cherished at all costs.

To really understand wishes, we must go to the experts, those who know more about wishing than the most ancient and shriveled guru—our children.

Digging Deeper: The Lifewishes

Wishes are an essential part of everyone's childhood. We more or less grow up with Santa Claus, the Easter Bunny, the Good Fairy, and other inventions of fantasy to which we direct our hopes for childhood rewards and delights. The unbridled imagination of the child can create the most marvelous of possible outcomes. We regard his wishes indulgently as charming reflections of youth. But there is function here as well. Wishing allows the child to make accommodations to a loss of control over external matters. In the first months after birth, the infant is the center of his own universe. His mother not only exists for him but is experienced as part of him. All the simple desires for contact and food appear to be automatically gratified. Gradually, in normal development, the child discovers his mother is not *him*, but an "other" apart from him. Some of his desires may not be met. Effort is now required to get gratification, and even the best of efforts may fail to bring the child what he wants. Reality has been introduced. The child learns the world is conditional, not always as pleasurable and rewarding as he once experienced it.

Yet the child yearns for the former state of affairs. He cannot recreate the Eden experience in which he was given constant attention and care. Instead, using his imagination he learns to tolerate his loss and the complexities of his future by wishing. He can wish the world to take any form. He can wish his baby sister did not exist, or that his father were a powerful king and he a prince. He can wish for a bugle, an ice cream cone, a dog. Wishing gives him a measure of imagined control and serves to make life more comforting when reality itself may be impoverished or stressful.

Indeed, many of us as adults unconsciously hold to these early wishes for the world to be fair, benevolent, and gratifying. We deny or avoid the harsher realities of human existence as a means—we think—of shielding ourselves from despair. In much the same way as the child, we want life to be easier, relationships more satisfying, work more meaningful. If we look closely beyond the obvious wish contained in every expectation, we will find a deeper, more encompassing hope. We can call this the "lifewish" because it is a desire for life or our relationship to it to be a particular way. For example, a woman is disappointed in the lack of common interests and attitudes she and her husband share. During their courtship they seemed to love each other so deeply that shared values and feelings were not an issue. Now that they are married, they continue to care for each other, but the sense of harmony has been lost. They are "out of sync." She had expected (wished for) their relationship to remain as it had been, but it has changed. The deeper lifewish in this situation is twofold: first, the desire for positive circumstance never to change, to live happily ever after; second, the wish for love alone to sustain a relationship.

Wishing: An Escape into Illusion

The deeper lifewish reflects an exaggeration or minimization of what really exists, in favor of what would really be preferable. It is an escape route from injustice, violence, insignificance, unhappiness. But as long as we want the world to be fair, we cannot help but feel disappointed when it is not. In wishing for the possibility of our own perfection, we are inevitably faced with the disappointment of our limitations. Important as our wishes are to our sense of future, they also create difficulty. When we believe in their possibility, we cannot assess reality properly. It is like watching a magician perform a sleight of hand. In order to believe in the magic we must see only the illusion created. Our perceptions are influenced by our wishes and contradicting information is screened out.

I once knew a man whose avocation was forecasting earthquakes. He predicted about twenty that never materialized. Then, on the twenty-first try, he hit the nail on the head. A small quake was recorded on the seismograph in the same month and in the general vicinity he had predicted. The man was heralded as a prognosticator of some merit. People forgot that twenty times he had forecast the event and twenty times he had been wrong. One coincidence was accepted as proof of his ability. People wanted to believe and so they conveniently disregarded the failed predictions. They filtered out contradictory data in order to make their wish come true.

When we invest in our wishes to the point where naked reality cannot touch us, we are labeled "psychotic" by the mental health profession. Most of us do not qualify. Our level of denial is more modest. If pressed we can see the world clearly. Catastrophic events, death, and disease often shake us into temporary lucidity. But it is relatively easy for us to hide in the lifewishes which had their beginnings in our childhood. These are the fundamental and deeper wishes which reflect our myths and illusions about life. And these wishes are reflected in our expectations. We have invested in them because we are loath to relinquish this deeper world view. To give it up would bring us face to face with sights and scenes we would rather not see. It would require that we confront the demons we have been long avoiding.

Attainable and Unattainable Expectations

Suppose a young track star is disappointed with his latest time for running a mile. The world record is about ten seconds under four minutes, and his time is close but not record-setting. He is disappointed because he had expected that he would set a new world mark in his last race. It may be possible to meet such an expectation if proper action is taken. That is, if the athlete prepares properly, works diligently, and receives good instruction, the anticipated outcome may, in fact, occur. But suppose the young man's disappointment is the result of an expectation that he will run the mile in two minutes, cutting the world record in half. Such an expectation is unreasonable and cannot be satisfied, regardless of action taken.

All expectation exists on a continuum of possibility. On the one end are those attainable with proper action. On the other are those impossible to meet regardless of action taken. This can be represented visually:

The Attainability Continuum

Expectation

Attainable——1——2——3——4——5——6——Unattainable

If I am disappointed with the amount of money I earn, we might say this is the result of an expectation that I will have X dollars at my disposal. Such an expectation belongs on the left side of the continuum, because I can exert control over my behavior and increase my dollar intake by working overtime on another job. If I am disappointed in how long it takes my body to rid itself of a cold, I have obviously been expecting faster recovery. This expectation belongs somewhere to the right of point three, since I can exercise only limited control over my recuperation by resting, reducing stress, and so forth. The cold will run its course with only minimal impact from my intervention. If I had anticipated reaching old age with a full head of white hair and I am disappointed with the fact I am balding, my expectation should be placed on the extreme right side of the continuum. The situation is not subject to change by action. No matter what I may choose to do, I cannot prevent my baldness.

Placing expectations on a continuum of possibility clarifies their reasonableness and defines the actions necessary to avoid disappointment.

There are many people who harbor expectations which are impossible to fulfill, yet they insist on maintaining them. There are others who have expectations attainable through some behavioral change, but they refuse to take the required action. Still others with midrange expectations assert that no action is necessary or apply the wrong remedy. All these people are doomed to a disappointment of their own making.

To put disappointment in an early grave, we must be ready to give up (de-invest in) our expectations or take appropriate actions to fulfill them. Success in this endeavor relies on our ability to assess possibility realistically, independent of the blinding influence of illusional wishes. We must see things the way they really are. This clarity demands from us the personal honesty and courage to challenge our myths and deeper lifewishes around which we have built much of our world view.

CHAPTER 2

The Roots of Disappointment

*One who has never been disappointed is either
a fool or a corpse.*
Graffito

Not all disappointments are equal. Some are devastating.
Others scarcely seem to matter. It all depends upon the
degree of emotional involvement in the failed expectation.
The greater the investment, the more severe the disappointment. Two factors determine the strength of that investment:
wish and time. The greater the underlying wish for an event
to occur, the stronger the pain when it doesn't; witness the
canceled wedding or the postponed vacation. Likewise, time
increases the level of yearning. The longer we delay, the
more urgent our expectation. Common desire held in check
becomes sexual passion. Waiting on line to see a play results
in heightened interest. But time increases the intensity of
expectation only up to a point, after which it begins to fade.
Expecting for too long creates tedium. An old Chinese prov-

erb states it simply: "Want a thing long enough and you don't."

We need some way to intelligently categorize disappointment—to distinguish between the feelings in response to a favorite disco closing for repairs and the realization that your son is not what you hoped he'd be. Arriving at a method for classifying disappointment is a bit like attempting to catalogue sand on a windy beach. It's everywhere to be found—in the most majestic locations and in the pants leg—but is one grain very different from another? Look closely. Even sand may be divided according to color, coarseness, and density. On examination, we can distinguish four types of disappointment: simple, chronic, developmental, and socially induced.

Simple Disappointment

This is the single, isolated experience of disappointment that accompanies us through our daily existence as we encounter the empty aspirin bottle, the late dinner, the uncooperative spouse. It may further be divided into two types: the "lightweight" disappointments most people could do without but accept as a consequence of living, and those significant, deep experiences of disappointment that wound and require recovery time, like the failure to get the job you really wanted or the breakup of a love affair.

Simple disappointments do not show a pattern. Each is different from the next, and there is no element of predictability. They are the result of faulty judgment, unrealistic expectations, exaggerated hopes, and chance.

It is with these isolated experiences of disappointment

that we are best acquainted. They are inevitable—by-products of the human capacity to fantasize and wish. Into every life some disappointment must fall. Most of us have few problems dealing with lightweight disappointments; we make adjustments without complaint. We are willing to concede our wishes once in a while. More significant disappointments, however, elicit emotional pain because our investment in them is greater. We care more deeply about the outcome of a particular set of events. Yet even this kind of distress is manageable, since it will pass with time.

All simple disappointments are subject to modification through insight and behavioral intervention. Whether we feel pain or successfully avoid it depends on our willingness to understand the nature of disappointment.

Chronic Disappointment

Far more difficult to eliminate are the chronic disappointments that drag on for extended periods and are repeated time and again. These are predictable experiences that follow a habitual routine. I have called such patterns "disappointment styles," because they are determined by enduring character traits which reflect the emotional history of the individual. If someone is continually and repeatedly disappointed in his children, job, or lot in life, we assume there is something in his personality that produces these chronic feelings.

Since disappointments are generally felt one at a time and memories of unhappy experience can be repressed, the chronically disappointed always fail to perceive the pattern of disillusionment in their own lives. Each new experience is somehow familiar, but unrelated to its predecessor. Clinical evidence shows that most of these people are repeatedly let down by the same sorts of things, but, blind to these recurrences, they are helpless to bring an end to their deflated feelings.

Put simply, chronically disappointed individuals don't learn from past experience. The feedback mechanism that enables the human being to avoid stepping in the same quicksand twice is in need of repair. For example, the grandiose individual who believes he is entitled to special treatment will be disappointed when he is assigned to an undistinguished office like his coworkers'. Yet he does not learn from this experience. On the contrary, that very same afternoon he is disappointed again when the boss vetoes his request for special time off, and once more that evening when the maitre d' keeps him waiting in line with everyone else.

Whether out of fear, disapproval, or anxiety, those who repeatedly experience disappointment have a psychological history that has produced expectations that are unrealistic, too absolute, too high or low. They need to readjust these expectations, but forces in their personality prevent them from doing so. Consider, for example, those individuals with impossibly high internal expectations who mistakenly believe that such standards are necessary to keep them functioning. Underneath their impossible demands for excellence, they suffer deep insecurity. They would rather experience the repeated disappointment provoked by their perfectionism than relinquish the rigidly high expectations which they believe keep them from sinking into mediocrity. The college student who refuses to submit a paper unless it is absolutely letter-perfect or the ad executive who demands that every client presentation be flawless illustrate this self-defeating style.

Habitually disappointed individuals feel depressed and lackluster most of the time. The experience of hope repeatedly followed by letdown is an emotional roller coaster that takes the joy and lightness out of life. Stuck in a morass from which they are seemingly powerless to escape, they develop a sense of impotence. As long as they remain prisoners of their own psychological history, they will continue to repeat the patterns that create disappointment.

Developmental Disappointment

As we pass through the various stages of life from infancy to old age, we find that certain disappointments are characteristic of a particular time of development. The young child, for example, innocent and unworldly, can be disappointed by virtually any event. He sees no limits on possibility. Life is mysterious and magical. Expectations are boundless. Disappointment is, therefore, frequent and traumatic. His mother, in her mid-thirties, is just beginning to fathom that many of her plans for the future will not be realized. Her alternatives are shrinking, and she must make either/or choices. Her disappointments are born of the adult developmental stage through which she is passing. Her father, in turn, must confront the disappointment of lost opportunities and plans never completed. He is faced with age-old questions: Is that all there is? How would I do it differently the second time around? Is life fundamentally disappointing? Each stage of the human drama brings its own disappointments as aspiration collides with attainable reality.

These developmental disappointments, so devastating in their impact, are important learning experiences. Contained within each is a challenge to our illusions about being. Rather than ignore or avoid them, we would do well to employ them to help us through the lifelong process of maturation. Like an austere teacher, birch switch in hand, they rap our knuckles with hard fact. They say, "You cannot live forever; opportunities are fleeting; life is short; we never get all that we want." They readjust our view of things by teaching us about the limits of possibility and the nature of life. The child cannot have every gratification. The grandfather has only limited time remaining. Developmental disappointment impels us to give up our dreams and make the most of what is. By doing so, we put our energy into living life instead of regretting its nature.

Socially Induced Disappointment

The shining, heroic American dream of economic opportunity, prosperity, and upward mobility is losing some of its luster. When few can afford to buy a house and still others cannot pay their skyrocketing utility bills, the familiar cultural mythology becomes an empty promise that mocks the national predicament. The combination of diminishing economic fortunes with the unwritten expectation that every generation will do better than its predecessor has produced a climate of disappointment and bitter readjustment.

The mood of the nation—the collective feelings of optimism or desperation—is affected by economic forces beyond individual control. These factors are generally obvious to the interested eye. Less noticeable are the covert social influences which manipulate our attitudes and perceptions. Advertising, television, and motion pictures exercise subtle sway. They spoon-feed us on their brand of fantastic expectation and dispose us to disappointment when those dreams don't pan out.

We are impressionable animals highly attuned to the variety of messages sent out to us through the advertising media. The constant barrage of gratuitous commercials is one of the hazards of life in the twentieth century. It is inescapable. Beautiful young men and women stroll leisurely through the woods to the background music of a dozen violins in order to induce us to buy an aftershave lotion or motor oil. No cares, no responsibilities, no oil on the fingertips. Such ideal representations suggest that purchase of the product will do the same for us. What's more, they persuade us that acquisition itself is salutary and meaningful.

In choosing to present imagined visions of life based on familiar myths such as the Triumph of the Little Guy or the Power of Love, Hollywood and the television networks cater to maudlin, commercial taste. Nothing fills the theaters like an updated morality play or a romance disguised in futuristic costume. The public will pay money to see them. What the public will not pay to see are films that portray reality. Few want to watch a slice of life. They prefer to escape it.

The themes and format of television and motion pictures affect our perceptions in much the same way as advertising. They encourage our own personal myths—which were in part created by the media—while inflating and romanticizing expectation. In presenting a world of illusion, the entertainment industry fills our unconscious with word pictures and ideas ungrounded in reality. By comparison, the real world seems two-dimensional and disappointing (more on this issue in Chapter Five).

Socially induced disappointment may result from major economic and political forces or from the covert influence of the media in our lives. Yet it hardly matters whether the White House, Madison Avenue, or Hollywood sets the conditions for feelings of disillusionment. The real issue is how to stay clear of these forces, a task that just may prove impossible. Perhaps the words of philosopher Alan Watts offer a solution: "Be in the world but not of it."

Is Disappointment Destiny?

As we consider the roots of disappointment, the inexorable question surfaces: Is the nature of life disappointing? A friend put it to me directly. "Why bother to look at specific disappointments? Life itself is pretty disappointing."

I asked him to elaborate, and he replied, "You're trying to solve the riddle of disappointment as if you could prevent it or help people to move through it, but what if the experience of life is intrinsically disappointing? What if life is not all it's cracked up to be? What if living itself is disenchanting?"

It was a jolting thought. Was I running around like a battle-crazed medic applying psychological Band-Aids and gauze to a problem that was simply inherent in life? Was repetitive disappointment built into a universal plan? If so, my remedies would be as effective as aspirin on left-handedness. Soberly, I thought more about my friend's observation. For some reason I remembered an old joke from my youth:

> A homely woman goes to a matchmaker who tells her about a wonderful man who is seeking a spouse. He's rich, kind, and looks like Cary Grant. Enticed by this prospect, the woman agrees to meet her new suitor in a café the next evening. She arrives early, barely containing her excitement. At the prescribed time, an old man shuffles in and sits down next to her. In her disappointment she bursts out crying. "You don't look a thing like Cary Grant."
>
> "You know something else?" he replies. "You don't resemble Gina Lollobrigida!"

The story demonstrates how clearly disappointment is a function of expectation. To the question "Is life itself disappointing?" we must in turn ask, "What did you expect?" Expect life to be fair, good to triumph over evil, the dead to rise again, miracles to save you, the wronged to gain redress, and you will feel constant disappointment. Life may be inherently too short or dissatisfying, but it is not intrinsically disappointing, since that condition is determined exclusively by what you anticipate. It is how you view life, not life itself, that creates disappointment.

"Don't expect Cary Grant," I said to my friend, "and you won't be disappointed when Woody Allen shows up."

"You have an interesting point," he replied, "but you're not considering the structure of life. As children we live in our imagination, with visions of endless choice and possibility. Life is like a huge menu. A child wants to eat everything it sees. We always ask children, 'What do you want to be when you grow up?' as if anything they choose is possible. We collude with their visions. And they say, 'I want to be a fireman, a brain surgeon, the first woman on the moon.' Anything. They believe anything is possible."

"But that's just the innocence of childhood," I retorted.

"When they grow up they have to adjust to the world."

"That's just the point. The nature of life is to begin with endless possibility and as the years go by all possibility diminishes. Time shrinks possibility!"

"Wait, you've gone too far," I declared. "Some of our dreams come true. In fact, it is only as adults that we *can* accomplish what we imagine. Children have to be satisfied with wishes only."

"It's true that you may reach a few of your dreams in adulthood," he responded, "but not many, compared to what you've imagined. To a child, the future is a vast expanse. But as you get older, time and energy—what you need to meet your expectations—keep diminishing. At thirty, you see that life is too short to achieve perhaps fifty percent of what you had wanted. At forty the figure gets even smaller, and so on. To make matters worse, you have less energy as you age. Managing a household, earning a living, and raising children are exhausting, even with an abundant supply of energy. Add to this the psychological responsibilities of adulthood and the physical problems of an aging body and you have a very heavy burden indeed.

"So there you have it. You start from a single point looking out at endless possibility. Your expectations are limitless. As you live on, fewer and fewer of those expectations are met. Time shrinks possibility. What you dream of is narrowed by diminished time and energy until you finish life with very few dreams at all. That's why life is by nature disappointing. You begin with promise and end with the cold limitations of reality."

I knew my friend was right as far as he went, but where he saw inevitable disappointment in the structure of life, I saw something else.

"It's true what you say," I replied, "up to a point, but you fail to take one human factor into account: the ability to learn from experience. Life may be an ellipse; possibility may funnel into limited reality. But if we know this will occur, we can make adjustments. The observation of a fact changes the fact. It may not be possible to eliminate disappointment, yet you can reduce it to a manageable level by accepting the natural life sequence you have just described. That means acknowledging that all your dreams cannot come true, and that human beings age and change. Maturation is a process of learning to accept life as it is. Holding onto expectations is merely forestalling the loss of a particular hope. Ultimately, repeated disappointment is a failure to accept the world without qualification. If you're willing to accept it as it is, then life does not have to be disappointing. There's enough excitement and wonder in living to justify relinquishing false hope."

Death and Taxes

Awareness of the elliptical nature of life gives us a perspective that prevents disappointment from getting out of hand, but it does not help us to eliminate it entirely. In later chapters, we will learn ways to reduce the level of disappointment in our lives and to deal effectively with significant experiences of letdown as they occur. We will explore methods for using disappointment to enrich our experience and prevent us from suffering greater disillusionment. But we must recognize that, like death and taxes, some disappointment is inevitable, a by-product of the foibles of human nature—the timeless patterns and quirks that are universal and historical. Embedded in civilization, these patterns are so commonplace that we are scarcely aware of them. Yet they explain why disappointment may shadow every human experience.

Taking Things for Granted: A friend recently told me of his plans to move for the third time in as many years. He lived in a lovely beach house with a magnificent view of the ocean. A labyrinth of hiking trails strewn with wild irises and poppies emerged from his front door. I asked why he might leave such a beautiful setting.

"Oh, I'm tired of it," he responded indifferently. "It was great when I first moved in, but now it's just the same old thing. I can't see it anymore."

I can't see it anymore. How accurate the statement. His eyes literally failed to look out at the ocean. He walked by the flowers without so much as a glance. He thought of his home as merely a place to lay down his head. Living in paradise, he might just as well have resided at the city dump. Nine people out of ten would have jumped at the opportunity to rent my friend's house, yet he did not appreciate its virtues.

Human beings have a curious capacity to take things for granted. The most exquisite diamond loses its luster with familiarity. The most compatible intimate becomes boring. Even miracles fail to astonish when they're commonplace! Repetition and time dull our sense of wonder. The thing that originally produces interest grows tiresome after repeated exposure. A favorite record played over and over becomes monotonous and dreary. Filet mignon consumed every day loses its savoriness. Even the fragrance of a rose stops arousing our sense receptors after only a few seconds.

We endow novelty with powers and attributes that it does not really possess. When a thing becomes familiar to us, the mystery we have projected onto it cannot be maintained. We see it from a more realistic perspective without the overlay of our imaginings. A new boy in class inspires fantasy in the schoolgirl until she gets to know him and he becomes just another kid. The young employee attributes maternal qualities to his older supervisor until he finds she is critical and unkind.

The irony in this idiosyncrasy of human character is that we are disappointed by the very things that used to excite us. The once new job, sexual partner, or leisure activity is now tedious. We feel let down rather than uplifted. Disappointment is a consequence of our expectation that an object or event will continue to provide us with stimulation regardless of how constant our contact. Unless we adjust our expectations accordingly, we will continue to feel deflated.

Anticipate boredom! But is this really a serious solution? Let me suggest another alternative: Maintain a fresh perspective on the commonplace by living life with contrast. If my friend had spent time away from his ocean home, he would have returned to it with "new" eyes. He would have seen it again as he did the first time. Some people take long vacations for just this purpose—to provide the distance necessary to see their life anew and appreciate it. Is this not recognition of the adage "Absence makes the heart grow fonder"? We value what we don't have. We take for granted what we do.

If the world were all red, we would not even know that red existed. Since everything would be that color, we would simply assume it was the nature of things. Introduce contrast in the form of blue, and we suddenly become aware that red exists. Now we can see it because it can be compared to something else. It is contrast that provides us with the antidote to taking things for granted and feeling disappointment. As the Chinese philosopher Lao Tzu wrote 2,500 years ago, "Under heaven all can see beauty as beauty only because there is ugliness. All can know good as good only because there is evil."

Time Traveling: After their children had left home, Amy and Richard, a professional couple in their mid-fifties, decided to take a trip around the world. Having lived in the same place for thirty years, they found the idea of globetrotting exciting and romantic. Here was an opportunity to view firsthand the cultural and natural wonders they had read about in novels and travelogues. They planned the entire trip carefully and thoughtfully, educating themselves about local customs, currencies, and places of interest. They studied languages, investigated climates, and planned extensive itineraries. Armed with the appropriate intestinal medications, they boarded the airplane and flew off to the Orient.

When they arrived at their first stop, they were excited and nervous. Hardly noticing the sea of humanity directly before them, they hurried madly from one place to another, determined to see everything in the guidebook. Each night they returned to their hotel tired and irritable. They weren't really having a good time, but they attributed it to jet lag. The second stop was much the same. Every day was a faultless replication of the itinerary planned back in the States. Something was not quite right, but neither of them could identify it. In spite of their uneasiness, they settled into a routine and ignored their discomfort. Besides, there was so much to see and photograph.

When they arrived home, they were fatigued and actually relieved. But then a puzzling phenomenon occurred. As they talked to their friends and family, they saw their vacation in a new light. It became an adventure, a thrilling experience. Through the distorting lens of memory, they had reframed it as satisfying and meaningful. The disappointment of the real experience had been filtered out. The vacation was a great success when seen from the perspective of before and after. Anticipating and remembering the event were better than the experience itself.

I call this sort of behavior "time traveling": living in the past or future, but avoiding the present. Instead of focusing attention on their feelings and the information supplied to them by their senses, time travelers are preoccupied with such questions as "What's next?" or "Isn't this similar to that time back in 1957?" Amy and Richard felt they were missing something, and they were: the present moment. They didn't take in what they saw. What was important was meeting the demands of an itinerary prepared three months before from a distance of ten thousand miles. Their immediate experience counted for little.

Focusing on the moment—what Fritz Perls called "living in the here and now"—means being aware of what is currently in front of you, awareness of self and situation. This is not a mystical or complex idea. Many people walk through life unconsciously. They eat without tasting, listen without hearing, look without seeing. They are preoccupied with thoughts of the past and future. If we had been there to ask Amy or Richard, "Did you enjoy your trip?" the most honest answer would have been, "I didn't really notice!"

Traveling through time, preoccupied with expectations or memories, prevents us from feeling the satisfaction (or discomfort) of immediate experience. We might say it blocks us from the immediacy of our own lives. A brisk morning walk by a clear mountain stream holds no thrill for an individual thinking about the business meeting last Tuesday. The executive immersed in thought is missing the encounter with the natural world—walking, smelling, observing, feeling. Consciousness of the temporal moment—"bare attention," in Buddhist terminology—is fundamental to a satisfying and healthy life. All neurosis is absorption with past or future.

Much of what we call disappointing relates to our inability to fully experience the "now." Without awareness of the present we merely swallow experience without savoring it. Even the most favored delicacy will disappoint the palate if it is not given sufficient attention. Living in the moment is a prescription for satisfaction as old as the Bible. King Solomon declared: "A man hath no better thing under the sun than to eat, and to drink, and to be merry"; the Roman poet Horace asserted: "*Carpe diem, quam minimum credula postero*" [Seize the present, trust tomorrow e'en as little as you may]; and the English poet Longfellow:

> *Trust no future, howe'er pleasant*
> *Let the dead Past bury its dead!*
> *Act, act in the living Present!*
> *Heart within and God o'erhead.*

As children, we are absorbed in the present moment without much concern for future or past events. Over time, the "cerebral wiring" becomes more complex and we find ourselves preoccupied with other concerns. This change is necessary and inevitable. There are lessons to be learned from the past and problems to anticipate in the future.

Present-centeredness is more an ideal than a natural condition in technological society. It takes discipline and awareness to achieve it, and it is doubtful if any but the enlightened could manage such pure consciousness continually. Even if we could, it is questionable whether our full interests would be served. Still, we can strive for a better balance between time traveling and the "here and now." To live more in the moment, thereby reducing our predisposition to disappointment, we must ask with regularity three simple questions of ourselves: What am I doing? What do I feel? What is it I want? The answers will both orient us to the present and give us greater awareness of ourselves.

Imagination—10; Reality—0: Imagination has no limits. It moves through space and time according to whim. Whatever the mind may invent, fantasy will deliver. Reality, by comparison, is limited by the physical laws of nature. Although they may sometimes be difficult to define (parapsychology gives us cause to wonder), the perimeters of possibility are generally accepted. Our bodies are finite. We require sleep, food, and water to survive. Our strength is limited by health and will. And so forth. The discrepancy between what we are and what we can imagine ourselves to be creates disappointment.

Fantasy contains its own perfection. The mind's musings are often idealized visions which real life cannot hope to duplicate. Eden, Shangri-La, Arcadia, Neverland, Atlantis, Laputa, and the Big Rock Candy Mountain represent only a few of the countless utopias that have captivated the human heart in every generation. Fantasy is faultless. All defects are removed by the dreamer. Reality is filled with blisters and pockmarks. History does not tolerate angels or utopias.

A patient of mine decided to build his own house, something he had always dreamed of doing. He pictured himself, hammer in hand, constructing the walls that would shelter his family from wind and cold. The sweat of his brow and the effort of his labor would be the foundation of this new structure. Like the frontier pioneers before him, he would literally construct his future.

You might guess what happened. The experience of building did not quite meet the relished expectation. Instead, my patient found himself immersed in the prosaic details of building codes, community architectural standards, and septic tank regulations. The pioneer vision was replaced by sore thumbs and a slipped disc. Reality had once again supplanted fantasy; disappointment was the consequence.

The words of a seventeenth-century Archbishop of Canterbury tell the whole story:

> In our pursuit of the things of this world, we usually prevent enjoyment by expectation; we anticipate our happiness, and eat out the heart and sweetness of worldly pleasures by delightful forethoughts of them; so that when we come to possess them, they do not answer the expectation, or satisfy the desires which were raised about them, and they vanish into nothing.

Empowering Objects: A couple determines that buying a house in the suburbs will correct the disturbing impasse in their marriage. Once settled in their new residence, they are plagued by the same relationship problems. The new house offers no cure for their alienation from each other.

A college sophomore wants a new sports car to enhance

his image (and combat inner feelings of unworthiness and inadequacy). After buying it, he discovers that even at 120 m.p.h. he feels bad about himself.

We often expect acquisition to provide magical remedies. We imagine objects have the power to furnish happiness and deeper satisfaction. As the couple and the college student soon realize, their solutions do little more than direct attention away from more significant dilemmas. The problems remain.

The issue is further complicated by the symbolic meaning we attach to particular objects. We see prestige, security, power, and respect in the procurement of material goods. The expensive automobile, the duplex on Park Avenue, the vintage wine all represent more than the possessions themselves. We imagine our association with them gives us standing and increases our merit. We hope somehow to be endowed with all the attributes which we project onto these objects. Like primitive people in the hill country of some distant land, we ascribe miraculous influence to the wooden thingumajig. (Ours are sold in the downtown department store.) A certain dress will make us irresistible. A movie camera will change our lives. Simply by obtaining such articles, we hope to capture their authority.

Of course, these expectations must end in some disappointment. Material acquisitions may make our lives easier and more comfortable, but they don't solve emotional problems or provide deeper satisfactions. Yet we continue to gather up and surround ourselves with possessions like squirrels preparing for the coming winter. We are particularly attracted to objects we can't possess. Offer a child A or B, but under no circumstances "C," and the choice is a foregone conclusion. Adults are no different. They ascribe great merit to the unobtainable and devalue what is more easily acquired. So predictable is this behavior that advertisers use it to manufacture interest in their products. By suggesting exclusivity and unavailability, they increase interest. We also place a halo over other people's possessions while devaluing our own. It's the old proverb "The grass is always greener. . . ." The context in which we view something influences our estimation of it.

Whatever the reasons for our attraction to material trappings—and they are numerous—it is important to keep our expectations regarding acquisition within the bounds of reality. Unto themselves, objects have no value beyond their immediate usefulness. When we expect them to help us avoid emotional pain or provide deeper satisfaction and meaning, we will always be disappointed. A new pair of shoes offers only a temporary remedy for depression. We would do better to address our problems directly.

The Deception of Appearances: In my clinical practice, I happened to be seeing two women who held similar sales jobs in the same company. They knew each other only superficially, but their relationship was cordial and friendly. Susan had occasion to remark how much she liked Pat. She emphasized what a happy, good-humored person she seemed to be. Pat, on the other hand, was taken with Susan's knowledge of herself. She thought of her acquaintance as "really in touch." The impressions Susan and Pat had of each other were the antitheses of what I knew to be true. Susan was an avoider, someone who would resort to almost any ploy to evade recognition of her true motivation. Pat wore a mask of pleasantness to conceal her discontent and sadness.

People are often deceived by appearances. They mistake

form for substance, assuming that what is displayed is a reflection of what exists below the surface. To complicate matters further, all of us play a game called "putting the best foot forward." This is a euphemism that encompasses a range of behavior from affectation to outright duplicity. We try to fool people into thinking we are better, richer, stronger, more loving than we actually are.

In spite of the fact that we're all in on this game, many of us seem to forget the other person is playing too. When we see someone who is "cool, calm, and collected," we often assume that the individual has no personal problems and is able to handle adversity without difficulty.

In the clinical setting, it is common for neurotic patients to compare themselves with others. Rarely is the evaluation accurate. Patients are all too familiar with their own shortcomings. They do not possess parallel information about others. As a result, they contrast their worst traits with the public image of strangers. And, of course, they end up disappointed in themselves.

Our society places great stress on appearances. Nowhere is this better illustrated than in the marketplace, where display is everything. American automobiles have always been long on exterior design and short on function. Only in recent years has international competition begun to force a shift in priorities. So much money is spent on packaging consumer goods that the process has become a subindustry in itself. The attractive label, the eye-catching container, the intriguing trademark are considered vital to successful marketing. In many cases the package is more important and more costly than the product. The general rule is "If it looks good, it sells good!"

Image and style are paramount in the political arena also.

Issues are secondary to presentation of self. What matters is the tone of voice, the choice of homily, the hair and jacket cut. Does the candidate look and act presidential? Is she a winner? Does he command enough respect? Social critics have argued that we now sell politicians at election time the way we merchandise washing machines—with thirty-second advertisements praising the virtues of the product. "He's a family man." "She's one of us." "He cares." The trend is to ignore the issues—certainly the most fundamental aspect of any campaign—and focus on personality. The candidate's winning smile counts more than her position on defense spending.

Disappointment and the deception of appearances are inextricably wedded. Eventually we discover that the candidate is just another person subject to the compromising pressures of political life. Or the new friend who seemed so easygoing initially is really compulsive and critical. All that glitters is not gold, is not even metal, but plastic! When we form judgments and expectations on the basis of outward show without consideration of their inner nature, we are walking a path that leads directly to disillusionment. It is important for human beings, who are so vulnerable to bright lights and tinsel, to remember that form itself has no essence. What we see on the surface is not necessarily what we find underneath.

The Right to Gratification

Mark is a bright, affable, forty-one-year-old technical writer at a company that manufactures personal computers. For eight years he has written instruction manuals for various software packages, and he is well regarded in this specialized field. In the past he has introduced numerous innovations in the standard manual; all have been accepted. This time, though, his suggested blueprint for a new method of organizing information has been rejected outright by his boss. Mark is shocked and angered. He starts coming late to work. He considers quitting. He is sarcastic and cynical at the most inappropriate times. His motivation diminishes. Everyone at work wonders what's wrong.

If we talked with Mark candidly, we would find that he is terribly disappointed. He feels hurt and betrayed by the boss's action which he experiences as a personal rejection. Something important has been taken away from him. With all his former success, Mark has come to expect that any idea he puts forth will be accepted. He considers himself special, and therefore privileged. The corporation is obliged to adopt his plan on the basis of his track record. Under it all, Mark has become full of himself, puffed up by his past glories. When his boss vetoes his idea, the bubble bursts. He reads the rejection as a statement of his personal worth. When it comes right down to it, Mark believes he is entitled to the satisfaction of his expectations. If they are not met, he feels personally diminished. His right to be gratified has been attacked. Like a child who doesn't get what he wants, he behaves impetuously.

If we believe—as did Mark—that we are special and deserve to be gratified, failure to get what we want feels like an injury to our ego. We bristle inside: "How can this happen to me? This treatment is unwarranted. I should get what I want!" At the heart of this prideful response is the narcissistic attitude that we deserve *not* to be disappointed. We feel entitled to have our wishes come true, and we deeply resent anyone or anything that comes between us and them. Self-gratification is seen as a right.

This is a pervasive attitude in our society today. We believe we are entitled to gratification by virtue of our birth. Is this not the message of the weekend gurus and the purveyors of instant enlightenment? Do we not believe that we should get as much for ourselves as quickly as possible? But who, in fact, can justify this claim to gratification? Certainly Mark could not. The fact that he had been successful in the past did not warrant the expectation that his ideas would be accepted regardless of their value or applicability. We have all been duped into believing that our expectations have prerogative!

Life is not in our debt. Our sense of entitlement cannot really be defended. Yet we have become comically serious about our wishes. We respond to their failure as if we've been shortchanged. We forget that wishing is fanciful, not earnest business. As a culture, we want what we want when we want it. Our disappointment in life itself is a consequence of the belief that we have an inalienable right to the satisfaction of our expectations.

CHAPTER 3

The Anatomy of Disappointment

The movements of expression give vividness and energy to our spoken words. They reveal the thoughts and intentions of others more truly than do words, which may be falsified. . . . These results follow partly from the intimate relation which exists between almost all emotions and their outward manifestation. . . .

Charles Darwin

The Six Stages of Disappointment

What does it feel like to be disappointed? I asked my ten-year-old nephew that question and received an instantaneous reply. "Disappointment is when you're playing Pac Man," he said with dramatic emphasis. "You've got the highest score ever and there's only one dot left on the board. And then, just at the moment you're ready to get it, the monster comes and eats the Pac Man. Boy, that's disappointing!" I've never played the game, but I understood the metaphor. The more intense the desire, the greater the expectation. And when the desire is at its peak and you're already planning the celebration, you get the bad news and groan in disbelief: "Could this really be happening? I was so close." A half-dozen or so exasperated thoughts run through your mind at rapid speed. But all you really notice is the end consequence—disappointment. Let's look more closely at the workings of this process.,

Suppose you have applied for a job with a large advertising agency. The salary is double what you're earning now. There are travel opportunities, a large office, and an expense account. To top it off, the possibility of further advancement is strong. Your potential boss will be promoted in a year, and her job will be up for grabs. Sounds wonderful, almost a dream. The interview went well. Your résumé was praised. Your chances are good. And you're going to hear the decision today. Naturally, you've got butterflies—more like migrating geese—in your stomach. The phone rings. It's Ms. A. from the agency. She begins, "I'm sorry to have to..." Your mouth drops. It's bad news. You didn't get the job. You feel terrible. Although you had told yourself not to "count your chickens," you had expected—underneath it all—to be hired. After all, they had praised your résumé and the personal exchanges were amiable.

Your first reaction is simply alarm—an *"Oh!"* response like an electric current running through the body. You are jolted by the delivery of discouraging news and your physiology is reacting by reflex. It's an unpleasant feeling—an orienting reaction to help you further process the information to follow. And it is quickly replaced by a sense of disbelief. You don't really accept the truth of the caller's statements although she couldn't be more coolly precise. She's told you the bad news but, for a few brief seconds at least, her words have not been fully acknowledged. You may think to yourself, "I can't believe this." Or "I can't accept this." Or "Is this really how it's going to be?" Your mind's rejection is similar to the experience of regurgitating spoiled food. The body says, "Get rid of it. It can't be processed." Likewise, the mind responds, "I don't want to process it." The denial defense cannot be maintained for long, however. In the face of indisputable reality, the bitter truth seeps in. Your thoughts turn in another direction. Perhaps you think about how hard you prepared for the interview, how you had to buy a new suit or rehearse for several hours. Suddenly the injustice of it all strikes home. You resent the forces that have prevented your expectation from becoming a reality. You feel frustrated and angry. You want to protest: "The nerve of those people. They don't know what they're losing." You might even take the whole affair as a slight and feel personally rejected and hurt.

Eventually you begin to feel a sense of loss. The objective fact—you have not been selected—sinks in. You lose energy. You feel fatigued and depressed. You'd like to withdraw to the safe confines of your bedroom and sleep away the next two days. You think to yourself: "I'll never find another job as good. . . . All that effort and I'm back where I started. . . . If only I had been hired." The realization of loss grows keener and you may find it hard to put it out of your mind. Dwelling on it produces feelings of resignation. The situation seems hopeless. Life is suddenly bleak. "All opportunities lead to a dead end, so why even try?" you say to yourself despairingly. Perhaps you even consider the undermining thought: *There's something the matter with me.* You go to bed but sleep doesn't come easily. The next day is plagued by list-lessness and intermittent feelings of purposelessness and resignation.

Many people seem to get stuck in this particular phase of the disappointment process. Dwelling on the failed expectation as if it were a material or tangible loss, they exaggerate its meaning and importance. Suddenly their whole world appears to have depended on this one specific outcome. All perspective is lost.

Time heals most wounds if we allow it. Several days later, failure to get the job no longer seems so important. You have accepted the unfortunate news and moved through your disappointment. But rather than feel elated or relieved you experience a curious absence of feeling. Other aspects of your life now seem more pressing. The disappointment fades into memory.

Until now you may have considered disappointment to be only a feeling, a specific emotion characterized by loss. After all, we commonly say, "I *feel* disappointed." However, it's more accurate to think of disappointment as a process broader in scope. Like the experience of grief, it has phases and direction. We might say disappointment is the struggle involved in moving from the failure of a desired outcome through the pain of loss to an acceptance of new circumstances.

Looking at our example again, we can identify six stages.

1. Expectation
2. Expectation Lost
3. Alarm
4. Resistance
5. Loss and Resignation
6. Acceptance

Of course, this is a rather neat and tidy model of the disappointment experience. Daily living rarely proceeds this clearly and simply. In actuality the resistance stage may follow the loss rather than precede it. Anger, hurt, and self-pity may flow out of the disappointed feeling, or the phases may be experienced in combination without clear delineation. But in general, the six stages portray the comprehensive process of moving through disappointment. Most of us will find it a useful road map when trying to gain our bearings in the midst of a disappointing experience.

Disappointment as Grief

In her well-known book *On Death and Dying*, Elisabeth Kubler-Ross identifies five stages through which the dying person moves in order to finally accept impending death: denial and isolation, anger, bargaining, depression, acceptance. These stages—with few exceptions—are markedly similar to those of the disappointment process. Denial and anger are early reactions in both cycles. Depression corresponds to the loss and resignation phase. Acceptance serves as the final resolution. Why should the reaction to disappointment appear analogous to the profound response to death? Surely the permanence and finality of the latter cannot be compared with the sometimes trivial nature of disappointment.

There is a natural progression of internal events when human beings confront any significant loss—no matter what the nature. We move through grief in a particular way. Most psychologists agree that there are no shortcuts. Disappointment involves a specific type of grief. Disappointed persons mourn for the death of a desire rather than for the loss of a parent or spouse. They had expected good weather for the celebration, but it rained instead. They anticipated their child would be accepted at Harvard, but she was refused admission. The significance of the loss may be small compared to the end of life, but it is loss nonetheless. To move to an acceptance of the new state of affairs requires predictable and patterned psychological maneuvers. Denial, anger, and resignation are preconditions necessary to fully absorb the new reality. For this reason, although death is far more tangible and momentous than disappointment, the human reaction is quite similar.

Yet logic tells us there is something unsound about comparing death with disappointment. Are we measuring apples against oranges? Not quite. It is more like comparing types of oranges or, in this case, types of losses. The differences are apparent. First, death is permanent and irreversible. Disappointment has no finality. What is lost can usually be gained at another place and time. And even if it cannot, the process of expecting continues. Unlike death, disappointment is only a setback on life's journey. Second, death is a concrete loss, whereas disappointment is merely the failure of an idea. Third, the magnitude of death dwarfs disappointment, even in chronic form. The existentialist philosophers call it the ultimate "boundary situation"—an experience that forces us to confront our own lives and place them in new perspective. Disappointment can help us to better understand the limits of possibility, but it rarely motivates a massive shift in the way we view our lives.

Disappointment as Stress

The mind and body function together as a whole. What we experience in our bodies affects what we think, and our thoughts have the power to produce physiological changes. Suppose, for example, you are to meet an old lover for lunch and you're anxious about the encounter. You wonder whether he'll still be attracted to you or if he carries resentment from the past. Such thoughts produce reactions in your body. Your breathing is shallow, you feel your heart beating rapidly, your hands are cold and sweaty. These alarming sensations in turn produce greater nervousness, more apprehension and doubt. Now you're certain the meeting is a bad idea. Perhaps he has an ulterior motive or wants something from you. Both mind and body are simultaneously involved in the discomfort. The mental event is a physical event. When an individual is disappointed, the same sort of dual reaction can be detected. Disappointment may begin in the mind, but it soon produces effects in the body.

Anyone who has ever been repeatedly disappointed knows that the experience is exhausting and debilitating. We might, in fact, call it stress-inducing, because the effort required to cope wears us down. It is fashionable in psychological and medical circles these days to acknowledge the relationship between stress and contemporary disease. High rates of the former produce increases in the latter.

Stress is credited with a role in many prominent psychological and physical problems, including peptic ulcer, colitis, bronchial asthma, hypertension, enuresis, migraine headache, general sexual dysfunction, insomnia, alcoholism, and a variety of neurotic and psychotic problems. Roughly fifty to eighty percent of all disease falls into this category of psychosomatic illness—disorders which are associated with or exacerbated by psychological factors.

Does disappointment contribute to this long list of ailments? Certainly, combined with other adversity, it increases a person's overall level of stress. By itself, however, most psychologists would probably rank it as only a minor nuisance. As a matter of fact, on the popularly used Social Readjustment Scale, which assigns numerical values to stress-inducing life events, disappointment is not even listed.

But suppose our earlier example of disappointment occurred in another context. You have been out of work for six months and are feeling some desperation because of precarious finances and significant loss to your self-esteem. In such a tight situation, the disappointment of not being hired would indeed create higher levels of stress. The unmet expectation might well be felt as a telling and final blow. The more desperate the context, the greater its destructive influence.

There is other evidence to indicate that the stress of chronic disappointment can produce physical and psychological problems. One of the most powerful experiences of disappointment is the one suffered by the repeatedly impotent male and his sexual partner. Nothing is more frustrating than continued unsuccessful attempts at coitus. Because anticipation and desire must necessarily be at high levels, the letdown created by failure to successfully complete the sexual act can be devastating. The male may feel frustrated and helpless, his self-esteem dealt a grievous blow. Partners usually feel equally distraught and disappointed. They may experience themselves as undesirable or unattractive.

Eventually, and often without discussion, both lovers collude in the avoidance of sexual contact. Neither wants to be disappointed yet another time. The scenario becomes a chronic cycle of expectation–disappointment–hopelessness, followed again by expectation.... It is an obvious example of how prolonged disappointment immobilizes and defeats.

Recently, studies at Loyola University's Sexual Dysfunction Clinic have suggested that the price of this disappointment is high. Sixty-two percent of the sexual partners of males with erection difficulties developed their own sexual problems over time. Many reported physical symptoms, including chronic backache and lower abdominal pain. Others became depressed and complained of feelings of rejection and sexual unattractiveness. Clearly, the relationship between chronic disappointment and the development of pathology is a direct one.

If disappointment works internally to produce unfavorable consequences for health and well-being, its more obvious effects on the anatomy of the disillusioned individual are also observable. Chronic disappointment is recorded in the body over time, revealed in posture and muscular-tension patterns. Less obvious are transitory disappointments which may be intentionally masked. Human beings are quite proficient at hiding their inner feelings at least temporarily and may reveal no outward appearance of letdown. Yet without these learned checks on expression, disappointment would likely be as easy to detect as it is in children who are more demonstrative than their acculturated parents.

Seeing Both the Trees and the Forest

In recent years there has been a renewed and lively interest in the psychology of the language and structure of the body. It is nearly six decades since a few maverick innovators in Freud's inner circle attempted to use physical techniques to serve the therapeutic process. Yet the mental health community has just awakened to the value of laying bare the psychological secrets contained in the human anatomy. The scope of that renewed interest can be measured by the arrival of at least half a dozen or so body-oriented psychotherapies which have gained current popularity, including Bioenergetic Analysis, Reichian Therapy, and Primal Therapy.

But what the examined body tells us is often difficult to deduce, especially for those not formally trained. Considering the complexity of the musculoskeletal system, the task seems overwhelming. The key to "reading" a body, to observe, for example, the chronic level of disappointment, is really quite basic. Look to the obvious. Notice the trees as well as the forest. Examine what you might normally take for granted: the expression in the eyes, skin tone, posture, movement, proportion, areas of tension. These characteristics tell us a great deal about the person we are observing.

Think of the body as a large piece of clay molded by experience and genetic factors. The muscles of the body, quite flexible in childhood, determine the basic shape of our physical structure. If those muscles assume a particular tension pattern for any length of time, it is likely to become fixed, affecting later physical growth. What causes the muscles to contract into a specific pattern? Generally, it is the highly charged emotional event. For example, if I experience defeat, my body will assume a physical posture that reflects that condition. My shoulders will slump, my pelvis will swing forward and tuck under. My arms will hang lifelessly. If I am defeated often enough, the pattern will be imprinted in the clay. Over the years, my body will tell its own history without a word from me. A person who is repeatedly disappointed looks that way. You can see it in the face, posture, and general attitude.

Denise: A Disappointed Body

To view the appearance of simple, deep disappointment in the body, let us consider the case of Denise, a computer analyst living in Los Angeles who has been conducting a long-distance relationship with Tony, a man she met while on a business trip to Chicago. At their first meeting, Tony had told her that his company planned to transfer him to California within the year. On the strength of this possibility, Denise had allowed herself greater involvement in the relationship. But she now reads a letter from Tony in which he tells her that his company has decided to keep him in the Midwest. He will not be transferred after all. Deeply disappointed, Denise moves through the six-stage process. What do we notice as we watch her?

Initially she reacts with alarm. Her body stiffens, and her face registers surprise. Her eyebrows rise, her eyes open wide; the upper eyelids raise, the lower relax. Her jaw drops, and her mouth opens slightly. These reactions are fleeting and momentary. They are quickly replaced by feelings of frustration and anger. The resistance to accepting her new state of affairs appears on her face. Her eyebrows are now drawn down and together. Her eyes become hard and penetrating. They have a narrow focus and the lower eyelids are tense. Her mouth is closed firmly, lips pressing against each other. Her body appears energized by protest. Her shoulders, upper back, and arms seem ready to move. Then, just as suddenly, these reactions are replaced by the dominant physical characteristic of disappointment: deflation. Think of a balloon filled to capacity with air. You have only to gently touch it and it bounces off your hand and into the atmosphere. Now imagine the same balloon without air. It is soft and lifeless. You hold it and it sags ingloriously in your hand. All elasticity is gone. This is analogous to what happens to the body during the fifth stage of the disappointment process. It diminishes in size, reflecting the experienced loss and dispossession.

Observing Denise we notice her shoulders drop and slump. Her head moves forward slightly. Her torso loses its upright quality and seems to collapse into itself. Her arms hang loosely at her sides. There is no vitality in her hands. She finds it difficult to inhale—her inspiration is quite literally lost. Her eyes appear tired and are cast downward. The inner corners of her upper eyelids are pulled up in sadness while the lower eyelids are raised slightly. There is less muscle tone in her face and throughout her entire body. She looks passive and drained—a disappointed woman.

Denise's physical reaction to disappointment is marked by three fundamental characteristics: deflation, energy loss, and restricted breathing. In recalling their disappointments, many of the patients I have treated comment specifically on these physical changes. Barbara, a lively thirty-year-old psychology graduate student, reported:

After my husband broke his ankle and our first vacation in two years was canceled, I felt awful. I had really needed to get away. I remember going shopping to try to lift my spirits. But each time I tried on something and saw myself in the three-way mirror, I felt worse. I looked tired and beaten. My body appeared just as I felt, collapsed and deflated. In a way I felt like I had just run a marathon, except I wasn't breathing very deeply. I had no idea I was so disappointed until the sight of my physical image clued me into the obvious.

And Janet, a successful forty-two-year-old real estate speculator, complained after she had failed to close a deal: "I was so disappointed I could barely lug my body around. I felt like a dead weight, tired and defeated. It was an effort to stand up straight. I thought to myself, why bother?"

This is the transitory, physical experience of simple disappointment. Even if the picture is obscured by the intentional inhibition of bodily expression, the characteristics of deflation, energy loss, and restricted breathing are recognizable in muted and evanescent form. But what happens when disappointment is a habitual condition? What is observable in the body of the chronically disappointed individual?

The Posture of Defeat

Take a moment to stand in a comfortable upright position. Close your eyes and consider what mood or condition your stance expresses. Does it seem defiant, removed, aggressive? Perhaps it is so familiar its meaning escapes you. If so, look in a mirror and exaggerate the postural tendencies until you can extract their significance. Now lock your knees, pull in your abdomen, square your shoulders, and puff out your chest. Hold your head erect and tuck in your chin. What state does this posture express? How different is it from your normal position? Notice that the simple act of standing in a particular manner remarkably influences your mood. The suggested military posture evokes feelings of invulnerability. The tension pattern underlying the stance gives you a sense of being armored, untouchable, and invincible. There is a noticeable absence of "soft" feeling.

Posture not only expresses feeling, it evokes it. Physical sensations influence what we feel. The mood expressed by a particular standing pattern is self-perpetuating. Posture responds to feeling, which in turn responds to posture. We tend to lock into one way of being upright because, once we are in it, the pattern reinforces itself.

We know that the primary physical experience associated with disappointment is deflation. Consider how a deflated stance would appear. The head droops forward out of line with the torso. The shoulders are rounded and pulled forward. The chest is deflated and falls into itself at the sternum. The abdomen collapses in the umbilicus region, creating the appearance of being foreshortened. There is a forward tilt to the pelvis, which is tucked under in the beaten fashion of a dog with its tail between its legs. The arms hang without vitality. The mood of the posture suggests defeat. The individual looks as if there is no future, only the constant repetition of past emotional losses. Think of a Picasso portrait from his Blue Period, or the melancholy strains of a Chopin nocturne. An individual who habitually stands in this manner will feel the hopelessness suggested by the position.

A basic and critical assumption of body analysis is that your relationship to the ground—how you stand on your own two feet—correlates with how you deal with the practical realities of life. If you're "out of balance," "up in the air," "heavy-footed," and so forth, you are "ungrounded." This means simply that you are standing in a way that prevents adequate contact with the ground. Your physical connection with the floor or earth is impaired in some manner. Like posture, groundedness shares a reciprocal relationship with psychological character. Those who stand rigidly or tentatively are psychologically ungrounded as well. Their link to basic needs, feelings, and sensations is disturbed. Unsupported by their foundation—the legs—they are also poorly rooted in their relationship to their body. This lack of connection either produces overintellectualized responses or impulsive, sometimes hysterical behaviors. Both are self-defeating and lead to high levels of anxiety and frustration. Ungrounded individuals do not see reality clearly. They depend on illusion to avoid recognition of their dysfunctional patterns.

One might predict that the habitually disappointed would be ungrounded. After all, their expectations for life are most often unrealistic and impossible to satisfy. In fact, chronically disappointed individuals often stand with their knees and ankles held rigidly, as if they were locked. The lower halves of their bodies may appear stiff and tense, without grace and strength. The legs may look a bit like stilts. There is no flexibility or ease of movement. The general impression is that they are bracing themselves against falling. This image is most descriptive. Because habitually disappointed individuals have been let down time and again, they stand rigidly as a defense against the inevitable fall into disillusionment. As long as their assessment of possibility is faulty, their stance upon the earth will reflect their insecurity and lack of rootedness.

The Despairing Face

The face is the most expressive part of the human body; it is also the easiest to mask. It may reflect our deepest feelings or appear as inscrutable as the classic psychoanalyst. It is capable of portraying a life story or simply the emotion of the moment. Mobile, changeable, complex, it is the principal means by which we identify ourselves and recognize others. Yet we rarely observe the detail of each other's faces. In conversation we may look at our friends, but only to the extent required to read their expression and react accordingly. We perceive agreement, hostility, boredom, and so forth, but we infrequently observe the character of the face. Like looking at a clock and noting only that you are not late without registering the actual time, we observe faces from a practical point of view. We extract what we need to know. The rest we ignore. Of course, there are exceptions to this practice; lovers gazing intently at each other, mothers observing their newborn children, artists scrutinizing their models. If I asked you to describe in detail the features of a friend's face would you be up to the task?

The face of the chronically disappointed person shows defeat and sadness. Signs of these feelings can be read in the eyes, forehead, mouth, and overall expression. None of the anger and protestation which we noticed in Denise's face is apparent. After so much accumulated disappointment, there is less resistance to conceding what has come to be regarded as a common experience. The disappointed face is drawn and tired. The muscle tone may be poor with noticeable deadness—a lack of energy—around the cheekbones. There is no brightness or gleam in the eyes, but instead the bleak quality associated with hopelessness. The mouth is tightly held, unable to risk reaching out and suffering another disappointment. Its corners are turned down in sorrow. The jaw is sometimes set in a fixed position, as if to hold back the need to cry. The forehead may be troubled and wrinkled, expressing a quality of world weariness.

The disappointed face reminds me of a visage from childhood: the unhappy clown whose countenance provides us with a caricature of disappointment that is simultaneously moving and disturbing.

Breathing: Sigh without Relief

The simple act of breathing is both commonplace and miraculous. We take thousands of breaths each day, with little awareness of the process. We leave it all up to the regulation of the hypothalamus and medulla oblongata. After all, they must be doing an adequate job or you wouldn't be reading this book right now! Breathing is an involuntary, unconscious process that is also subject to volitional control. We can change our breathing patterns—the rate and cadence—by intention. We can hold our breath for some length of time, or we can pant rapidly. Many variations are possible. When we inhale oxygen into the lungs, the diaphragm, a thin, muscular, tendinous sheath which separates the abdomen from the heart and lungs, descends to allow for expansion of the rib cage. At the same time the spinal column elongates and rocks the pelvis forward. During exhalation the opposite movement occurs, with the diaphragm ascending and pushing air out of the lungs. Full respiration creates a wavelike motion throughout the torso.

There is a direct relationship between our breathing patterns and the intensity of our feelings. When breathing is minimal and the diaphragm and muscles around the rib cage are tense, we experience less sensation and emotion. We feel cut off from part of ourselves. Full respiration creates the opposite situation. Our bodies are replenished with oxygen. We are sensitive to sensation and feel energetic, alive, and mobile.

Breathing patterns have a tendency to become fixed over time, but they are frequently modified by immediate experience. A terrifying movie will cause most of the audience to hold its breath, thereby restricting oxygen intake. A quick sprint to get out of the rain will charge the body with oxygen and may release tension in the diaphragm. Similarly, the experience of disappointment has its own effects on breathing. The chronically disappointed individual shows constricted respiration. His diaphragm does not move easily, and he may have some difficulty inhaling. This condition reflects the generally dismayed and resigned attitude that accompanies disappointment: It's just not worth the effort. Full respiration is an assertion of one's right to exist. It is a statement of vitality and security. Disappointed individuals are too defeated to accomplish such an action, nor would they want to. Breathing fully would bring them into contact with their dissatisfaction. Limited respiration helps them to restrict the degree of feeling they experience.

On the biological level, disappointed individuals are caught in the expiration phase of the breath cycle. It is as if they are stuck in a brief but repeated sigh. Inspiration then becomes taxing because the deep-seated tension in the muscles between the ribs hold the chest in a deflated position. The defeat associated with disappointment creates a restricted breathing style that reinforces itself. But like posture, these self-perpetuating patterns can be changed through awareness and intention.

As Kazantzakis reminds us in *Zorba the Greek*: "As I now knew the name of my affliction, I could perhaps conquer it more easily. It was no longer elusive and incorporeal; it had assumed a name and a shape, and it would be easier for me to combat it...."

CHAPTER 4

Life Cycle Disappointments

> *To grow older is a new venture in itself.*
>> Goethe

When my friends and I were studying developmental psychology in graduate school, we used to tell the following anecdote:

> A middle aged man is so worried about losing his hair that he feels depressed and anxious most of the time. His appetite falls off, and he has difficulty getting to sleep at night. In desperation he seeks professional help.
>
> His physician takes one look at him and decides he is too run down. For his own good, he needs to reduce the stress level in his life. The doctor recommends a long vacation in the Bahamas, a job change, and a bottle of tranquilizers.
>
> Unsatisfied, the man visits a psychoanalyst, who concludes that he's suffering from unresolved Oedipal feelings reawakened by his wife's interest in a new career. He advises a four-year course of analysis, with sessions three times a week.
>
> Feeling worse than ever, the man goes to see a psychologist,

who listens to his complaints and declares, "You're afraid of confronting your mortality and acknowledging the loss of your youth. There is only one solution. Wear a hat!"

As we move through the life cycle, all of us—as a normal course of our development—must contend with the struggles inherent in each of the different phases. These "crises" of development are sometimes mistaken for signs of deeper and more profound problems. Our balding friend is suffering only from the adult growth pains inherent in the midlife passage. It is important for us to recognize these development stages so that we can move through them more comfortably.

Not surprisingly, it was Freud who offered the first systematic theory of human development. He emphasized that the important psychosexual periods of growth were centered exclusively in childhood. His five stages—oral, anal, phallic, latent, and genital—are still widely accepted among clinicians today.

In contrast, developmental psychology offers another perspective: that the individual changes throughout the entire lifespan from conception to death. Adulthood is not a personally stagnant period of forty-four years (ages twenty-one to sixty-five), but a succession of life phases, each with its own specific challenges. Indeed, the entire process of maturation requires struggling against the counterforces of stagnation.

With the exception of Gail Sheehy's widely read book *Passages*, which popularized this perspective, developmental psychology has rarely been in the public eye. Yet over the years it has become a powerful intellectual force, encompassing a diverse body of knowledge, from the theories of mental evolution propounded by pioneer psychologist G. Stanley Hall to the "constructionism" of Swiss researcher Jean Piaget.

In recent years, the writings of Erik Erikson have particularly influenced the developmental point of view. In his seminal work *Childhood and Society*, Erikson set forth eight life stages, each containing a "psychosocial" crisis in which two conflicting tendencies within the individual are reconciled. Adolescence, for example, is seen as a period in which young people struggle to define themselves. It is the confrontation between the inclination to develop identity and the concern with how one is seen by others that characterizes this phase and gives it a tumultuous quality.

Erikson's basic assumptions are helpful in understanding our own changes. They can be summarized in this way:

1. Human development reveals itself through symptoms of apparent discord; yet it is this struggle between opposite tendencies that produces maturity.

2. The process of change is continuous throughout life and does not cease once adulthood is reached.

3. Individuals move through growth stages when they are ready, not according to a strict chronological timetable. For some people the issues faced during middle age may come a decade later than for others.

Developmental Disappointments

The stages of the life cycle are characterized not only by the struggle of conflicting tendencies but also by the appearance of disappointments specific to a particular period of life. Since each new stage of life demands that we surrender some of the comfortable behavioral and attitudinal patterns of the previous stage, there is always a feeling of loss and disappointment accompanying each change. Expectations of adolescence don't fit easily into young adulthood, and so on up the developmental ladder. Thus the thirteen-year-old—although eager to assume adult privilege—is sorely disappointed when forced to relinquish the special protective relationship with parents.

Beyond this point, however, there are disappointments built into the process of acquiring worldliness. As we age, more of our dreams and wishes are challenged by the accumulation of life experience. At thirty-five it is harder than it was at sixteen to hold onto the illusion that justice governs human relations. At sixty-five such a wish is already dead and buried. The loss of these illusions produces a sense of disappointment as what we expect from life is constantly undermined by the tough lessons of experience.

We will investigate inherent disappointments within six life passages: infancy/childhood, adolescence, young adulthood, early middle age, middle age, and later adulthood.

Infancy/Childhood

From the moment of conception through preadolescence, the child shows unequaled growth intellectually, emotionally, and physically. If everything proceeds smoothly—and this is a big "if"—the young organism will acquire before puberty a basic sense of trust, self-control, independence, purpose, and competence. This is not an easy period of development. Beginning in the first months of life, the infant is caught in a dilemma between the desire for continued and repeated gratification and an equally relentless demand by the parents to behave in a socially acceptable manner (the conflict between instinct and culture). In struggling to find some resolution, the child uses fantasy as a means of providing security. Wishes allow a measure of imagined control over circumstance. And in the child's view of things, wishes and expectations are virtually the same thing.

Disappointment flourishes in childhood for just this reason. Because the child's expectations are colored by fantasy without the counterbalance of life experience, they are poorly conceived and frequently go unmet. The failure of an expectation is felt as a tangible loss by the young, who have no sense of perspective and endow their wishes with symbolic meaning. This is why the smallest frustration may evoke as grand a reaction as a major loss.

The vast world of illusion which we encourage in children through "Disneyesque" or synthetic folk tales, myths, and stories also creates the preconditions for disappointment. We teach children to believe in miracles, happy endings, gratification of true desire, good and evil, Santa Claus. These ideas, which represent our own deeper wishes for a sweeter and more benign reality, are used to maintain and nurture the innocence of the young. In their own way they provide the child with reassurance against imagined fears and pain. The developing ego is not yet ready to face the true nature of the world. Reality must be accepted gradually, paced to the individual's growing internal strength. The problem, of course, is that in protecting the fragile burgeoning self, we cause other problems. When the five-year-old discovers there's no such thing as Santa Claus, she feels let down and shaken, and wonders what else is not true. Still, such disappointments rarely scar. There's a resiliency in childhood that enables the young to tolerate most disillusioning experience without unfavorable consequence.

Beside the usual disappointments with which every parent is familiar, there are four unavoidable and developmentally linked experiences that *do* have a major impact on the child. These involve restrictions on gratification, incest, and Oedipal desires. The impact occurs when the child discovers that:

1. Gratification is not always available. You can't always get what you want when you want it.
2. Gratification is highly conditional. You must behave in a certain manner to get what you desire. Sometimes even the "correct" behavior doesn't produce the wished-for outcome.
3. An exclusive physical and emotional relationship with the mother is prohibited (no incest).
4. An exclusive relationship with the opposite-sex parent, shutting out the same-sex parent, is prohibited.

Adolescence

Extended in Western society by the delay of marriage and the requirements of higher education, the period of adolescence contains both the lofty fragrance of freedom and the mildewed odors of childhood dependence. It is a transitional period with its own values, lifestyle, and peer pressures, but it often appears as a way of life unto itself. Few of us would choose to relive our adolescence. Indeed, we want to forget the humiliations and cruelties suffered through youthful ignorance and excess. We know just how difficult a period of time it was. Struggling to develop a sense of independent identity, yet still requiring the emotional support provided by the family, adolescents are caught in a bind. They have an incessant and powerful urge to be free, but they lack the ability and maturity to handle full responsibility.

This is a chaotic time in the life of the individual. Young people must contend with innumerable pressures. For one thing, their bodies are changing rapidly and these changes create all sorts of doubt and confusion. "Who am I?" is no longer a psychological question, but a physical one as well. In response, teenagers experiment by "trying on" various roles and appearances. They may dress and behave like heroes one day, bizarre "punks" the next. Or they may act promiscuously, wear "glamorous" clothes and an overabundance of makeup. Such experiments are indirect attempts at addressing the troubling and persistent issue of identity.

Disappointments in adolescence are varied, encompassing the general areas of concern in this period: peer-group acceptance, biological changes, restrictions on initiative and choice. Underlying all these difficulties is the uneasy issue of identity.

Peer-group disappointments revolve around failure to be recognized as desirable, attractive, and, therefore, worthwhile. These are the typical teenage disappointments portrayed in the popular media. Exclusion from the "in" group, unrequited love, and the disloyalty of friends receive a great deal of attention because the issues of popularity and worth are closely connected. Teenagers, uncertain of just who they are, often interpret rejection experiences as indications of their value.

Disappointment with one's newly emerging physical self is usually unspoken, but anyone who remembers adolescence knows the importance of this issue. Anxiety about height, weight, breast size, genital development, and facial characteristics is heightened. Rapid growth, which produces physical and psychological awkwardness, sometimes misconstrued as permanent, creates additional doubts. Comparison of one's physical attributes with those of a favorite hero also increases the level of disappointment.

To the ten-year-old who mimics his older brother or simply observes the externals of adolescent life, the period seems ideal. I have rarely talked with a young person who was not looking forward to the teenage years, with their appearance of freedom, self-regulation, and excitement. When the ten-year-old grows up, however, he discovers that the free and easy attitude is only one part of the story. Life isn't as much fun as it appeared to be. There are pressures from school, peer group, and parents. Freedom is conditional and frequently restricted; responsibilities increase and, with them, disappointment.

Although the adolescent looks like an adult, he or she is very much a youth in the eyes of those in authority. This situation is, perhaps, the greatest disappointment of the period. It leads to a feeling of being misunderstood—a theme which permeates the songs and myths of the subculture. To the teenager, restrictions on freedom are an arbitrary affront to a growing sense of adulthood. To the parents, they are a recognition that their offspring are not mature enough to handle the responsibility of self-regulation. The battle between restricting adult and freedom-craving adolescent goes on in every generation. The result is a continual series of disappointments rooted in a false expectation of unlimited freedom and privilege.

Young Adulthood (20 to 32 years)

The early part of this life phase is filled with promise, aspiration, and possibility. Consequently, it is heavily weighted with anxiety and relatively free of disappointment. No longer shackled by the restrictions of childhood and the ambiguity of adolescence, young adults are in search of a direction and purpose, a mentor or guide, and a relationship that can deepen and provide security. This is a time when the focus on "me" is broadened to an emphasis on "we," when isolation and loneliness are replaced by community and friendship, and when participation in society brings satisfaction. Freud was once asked what distinguishes the healthy from the neurotic personality. He replied that it is the ability to love and to work. These are precisely the struggles of this period in the life cycle—to find meaningful work and relationships.

In *Passages* Gail Sheehy suggests two other urges in this stage: to build firm, safe structures for the future, and to explore and experiment, keeping all things tentative. The relationship between these opposing inclinations gives the phase its particular character, and reveals something about the specific needs of the individual who follows either extreme.

Young adulthood is still a time of unchallenged illusion. There is as yet not enough life experience to dampen one's expectation of an "anything's possible" tomorrow. The adult role is too new and probationary, too prejudiced by the nervousness of first experience to allow for the farsighted perspective that comes with age. Particular illusions carried from childhood begin to surface in this phase. Sheehy points out three:

1. Willpower overcomes all.
2. There is one true course in life.
3. I'm unique.

To the young person putting down first roots in an adult world, not many things are certain. Jobs may come and go. Money is in short supply. Love appears and floats away on the evening breeze. But through it all, one idea is sustaining: *I will—by virtue of my desire—persevere. My will can conquer adversity*. This is the attitude of the early and middle twenties. It is the only thing unequivocal at a time when everything else is uncertain.

Hand in hand with this belief goes another less confident proposition: *There is one true course in life. I have only to find it*. Indeed, this is the task of the young adult who is faced with many "first" choices in the twenties. The idea that there may be countless roads from A to B is threatening because it creates greater uncertainty. To erase the anxiety that comes with vagueness, young people try to create certainty where it does not exist. In doing so, they may become enamored of the irrefutability of gurus or the demand of "shoulds." "I should live a life of social significance." "I should get proper training while I'm still young." And so forth.

Individuals in this period are also convinced that they have arrived at their choices through a process purely of their own making. In defining themselves through their actions, they rarely see that their preferences may be a reaction to Mom or Dad, or that they are based on internalized family values or societal injunctions. They view their decisions as singular and uncontaminated, made only with conscious intent. In this sense, they see themselves as unique.

Disappointment during the early part of this stage is less common. Great expectations exist intact, unchallenged by failure. If disappointments are experienced, they are generally cast aside. There is so much possibility that the loss of one or two anticipations is trivial. This is a time of inflation; anxiety about the future is counterbalanced by the loftiness of one's own illusions. Doubts are hidden beneath resolve. Somehow a happy ending is seen as inevitable despite surrounding evidence to the contrary.

In the latter part of this phase, however, disappointment becomes more common, particularly disillusionment in self. By the late twenties and early thirties, the wide-open promise of an unparalleled future begins to fade and the first extended look at who we are is honestly taken. Up until this point, confrontations with our identity have been secretive glances colored by hopeful deception. But the repetitive patterns of behavior and feeling are now too noticeable to avoid, and the protective environments of home and school no longer obstruct us from clearly seeing ourselves. In effect, we come face to face with who we have become after the long incubation of childhood and adolescence. It is as if a veil has been lifted from our inner vision and we are now able to perceive without distortion. Paula, a thirty-one-year-old journalist and editor for a weekly county newspaper, spoke about this experience in her life:

> It's hard for me to admit just how little I knew about myself until a few years ago. I thought I was a pretty healthy person with no real psychological problems and a positive outlook on life. I considered my family to be rather normal—no hangups worth mentioning. No problems with Mom, just an occasional disagreement. I thought my sisters felt the same way, although we rarely talked about the family.
>
> Then, a few years ago, I started to realize I was having problems with my close relationships. I used to blame it on the men I dated. This guy wasn't trustworthy, so I couldn't get close to him. That one had problems with commitment. Another reminded me too much of Dad. After this went on for a while,

I began to see that even though these men were not right for me, I was still choosing them. I knew they were afraid of getting close, but maybe I was too. Maybe that's why I chose them in the first place—so I wouldn't have to commit myself.

I began talking to my sisters about this and about our family. I realized how much I'd forgotten about what happened in our home. We all agreed it wasn't a bed of roses. It wasn't the happy time I pretended it to be for so long. I feel sad about that. Sad that it wasn't the way I wanted it to be.

Like other individuals in the latter part of this life phase, Paula has surrendered self-protecting myths and inauthentic feelings ("I have no problems; it's everyone else's fault") in order to face her real nature. She recognizes her fear of commitment because the pattern has occurred too many times to ignore. Most of us would like to maintain our self-fictions, but by our early thirties we have had enough life experience to recognize our neurotic sexual attitudes, self-defeating and self-deprecating behaviors, poor relationship choices, and work-related difficulties. With our eyes opened to these patterns we begin to feel frustration and disappointment in self. We had expected the situation to be different. We had wanted to turn out closer to the ideal each of us carries in the back of our minds. Yet by denying our dysfunctional behaviors, we cannot hope to eliminate them. Ultimately, it is the acknowledgment of disappointment in ourselves that helps us to make the personal changes necessary for the transition to middle adulthood.

Unfortunately, the depth of our disillusionment is just beginning to be known. The notorious "midlife crisis" is about to ensnare us and shake our very foundations.

Early Middle Age (33 to 45 years)

I first met Peter at a party ten years ago, just after he had finished his residency in internal medicine. Ironically, we spoke then about the great possibilities that lay before us as we both embarked on new careers. Peter had followed the life script that had been laid out for him many years before. He had always worked hard, gotten top grades, gone to the best schools, and achieved whatever goals he had set out for himself. A successful medical career was the next challenge.

Just after college Peter married a woman with a similar middle-class background. She had grown up in the same sort of environment and shared his values and world view. While he was in medical school, she assumed the role of bread-winner. But as with so many student marriages, the stress of long hours of study, the time apart, and the different worlds in which they lived took their toll. They began to fight continually. Positive feelings of love and affection were buried under long, exhausting arguments. They debated anything and everything, from politics to the effectiveness of kitchen appliances. When Peter graduated from medical school, the marriage broke up.

For over a year, the effects of all that struggling weighed heavily on him. He became cynical and world weary. Mis-ogyny leaked out from the reservoir of hurt and resentment. Gradually, he reassembled himself and, focusing on his med-ical training, he got on with his life. A few years later he married another woman, very different from his first wife. She was the physical opposite—tall and blond—with a vastly different personal history.

Peter's career as a physician went along with routine

smoothness. He was successful, as he had been at most things in the past. He and his wife had two children. They bought a large house with a lovely backyard—plenty of room for a garden, a large swing, and a treehouse. They had no financial problems. Peter's practice nearly doubled within two years, and his wife worked as a consultant to several computer companies.

During this time, he seemed to settle into his life. He joined a number of local organizations, took responsibility for the garden and landscaping around the house, spent time with his children, and worked long hours teaching and treating patients at one of the local hospitals. To the outside observer his was a life to envy. No major problems. No economic worries. A good marriage.

Peter could not tell you precisely why, but in his late thirties he began to lose interest in his relationship with his wife. They were relatively compatible. They rarely fought, as he had done so often in his first marriage, and they shared mutual interests—the house, the kids, the management of their busy lives. The only thing Peter could say with certainty was that passion no longer existed between them. Perhaps it never had, but he was now very aware that he felt bored. Things were too predictable. He knew her opinions before she expressed them. He knew what she would wear, what words she would use to describe an experience. He felt he understood too much about her; the mystery of their differences had died.

When he reached his early forties, the feelings of boredom which he had tried to ignore began to spread to other parts of his life. He was bored with the same routines at work, the same faces and tasks. He was tired of getting into his car each morning and driving identical roads to the same destination. He was uninterested in his conventional friends and their drab conversation:

> Everything I do feels as if I've done it before, and not just once or twice but hundreds of times. My life is a permanent *déjà vu*. There's no excitement anymore, except for my kids and the thought of escaping to some exotic paradise. I thought there was more to life than this. I believed that if I worked hard I would be rewarded and those rewards would keep me going. Well, I've gotten what I wanted but it doesn't interest me anymore. It doesn't seem to matter. I almost feel like asking, "What was the struggle for?"

Peter's story sounds familiar. It should. He is not alone in his feelings of tedium and alienation. The midlife impasse of the middle thirties and early forties is as predictable as the politician's promise. If the last half of young adulthood is a time of disappointment in self, then this is a period of disappointment in life.

According to Erik Erikson, the challenge of the middle adult phase is to create a synthesis, pulling together all aspects of one's life into a meaningful whole. Productivity and creativity combine with feelings for others and culminate in the development of "generativity"—concern for guiding the next generation. When this characteristic fails to evolve, the individual stagnates, pseudointimacy develops, and there is a sense of personal impoverishment. The midlife crisis reflects the struggle to establish meaning in one's existence and prevent stagnation and ennui.

As we move steadily into middle age, several things happen. We settle into a "long-term" lifestyle that has an appearance of permanence. Up until now, there have been regular and frequent adaptive changes demanded by life's exigencies. The structure of the educational system, for example, created a major upheaval every four years or so from high school to postgraduate or professional training. Then too, there were other urgent matters: the jockeying for the right job, the search for the compatible life partner, the purchase of the new house, the birth of the first child. By the mid-thirties most of the natural "beginnings" in life have been encountered and a measure of stability is introduced. We have found a course to follow and have committed ourselves to it. The period of preparation is over. It is time to live.

With this settling-in experience comes our first extended contact with repetition and monotony. Each day looks very much like the last. Rituals and patterns become firmly established. Constancy produces security, but it also creates tedium. Even arenas of challenge and excitement like work and sex can become prisons of redundancy.

Repetition in early middle age produces a sense of emptiness. We get restless. We feel trapped. We notice with regret that the fervor of our youth is gone. With surprise we recognize our corruptibility for the first time. We begin to use the word "jaded" in describing ourselves.

This is also a period when we encounter the initial signs of our mortality. As we move beyond the halfway point, the symbolic significance of this chronological juncture is not lost on us. There's not that much time left. "Where did it all go?" We notice as well that our physical beauty and endurance begins to fade. Our faces show the strain of too little sleep and too much anxiety. The character lines are firmly and obviously etched. The wrinkles encountered each morning are permanent fixtures in the flesh. Our bodies also display signs of sagging. Tissue accumulates in the wrong places. Bulges no longer disappear with moderate dieting.

The recuperation rate from misuse and overindulgence lengthens dramatically. The pulled muscle takes longer to heal and longer to relax. All these indications are concrete evidence that physical being is finite. Our bodies will not go on forever. Will is no match for time.

Beyond these facts, we are also faced with the realization that our alternatives are shrinking. As youths, we had numerous paths to take and seemingly all the time in the world to take them. Now we are saddled with responsibilities, tangible physical limitations, and fewer years in which to accomplish anything. Our options are reduced geometrically by these considerations. The naive, world-embracing optimism of the adolescent, which could declare without self-consciousness, "I'm going to be president of a large corporation, have three children, and help the poor!" has been reduced to a more modest level in keeping with midlife realities.

Taken together, all these factors—repetition, ennui, mortality, shrinking possibility—produce severe disillusionment with life. Indeed, this is a period of great disappointment that often leads to depression. Some individuals experiment with sexual promiscuity, imbibe large quantities of alcohol and drugs, or throw all caution to the wind and flirt openly with death (parachuting, car-racing) to escape from the distress. Generally, such attempts create other problems of even greater severity.

The disappointments of midlife revolve around one central theme which will be repeated once more at life's finale: "Now that I know what it's really about, I'm disappointed that that's all there is." The other disappointments of this period in love, work, family, level of accomplishment, and loss of beauty and youth are merely variations on this theme. Midlife disenchantment is essentially a crisis of disillusionment. We have lived over fifty percent of our allotted time only to find that the illusions we have treasured since childhood have all been maimed or destroyed by uncompromising reality. We plaintively ask, "Is that all there is?" because what we have experienced doesn't measure up to what we expected, what we imagined, and what we wished life would be.

The middle-adult passage is a period in which we redefine our expectations, substituting a wiser, more tolerant and accepting perspective for the romantic and illusory hopes of youth. Those who make it successfully through this phase have allowed such an adaptation. Perhaps they have changed careers, developed new interests, encouraged their creative selves to flourish. What is most important is that they have established authentic goals for themselves—independent of the programmed expectations of their childhood and society—and that their new direction is rooted in a mature knowledge of possibility. Readjusting expectations is the key to a successful midlife transition.

Middle Age (45 to 64 years)

This period of life, formerly viewed in combination with early middle age, has been considered only recently as a separate entity by developmental psychologists. With the gradual increase in life expectancy and the new cultural concern for the aging process, it has emerged as a critical phase in the life cycle, with its particular satisfactions and its characteristic problems and disappointments. "On the wrong side of forty," but far from dotage, individuals have by this point developed a repertoire of behaviors to cope with most life challenges. Indeed, according to both popular myth and established fact, it is men in this age group who run the country, determining our collective future in the cloak and board rooms nationwide.

In terms of money and privilege, middle age is the prime of life—a time when power and ability are at their peak. Income is at its highest level. Unemployment rates are lowest, and the percentage of families below the subsistence level is well under the national average. Likewise, the number of families living in homes they own is higher than in any other age grouping.

With the midlife crisis safely behind, this stage is distinguished by renewed steadiness and permanence. Mobility decreases. Roots grow deeper. Life patterns become entrenched. Between 1975 and 1980, only twenty-seven percent of those in this life phase moved their primary residence. This figure represents half the rate of those under forty-five years of age. Although on the rise, the number of divorces is also less than the national average. After years of being coupled, the motivation to live alone or to start again in a new relationship drops off. Clearly, these are years in which one settles into a stable and patterned existence without disruptive changes.

But these are by no means problem-free years. In fact, depression, alcoholism, and suicide are major concerns in the middle-age population. The death of one's spouse, the empty-nest syndrome, the fears associated with retirement, menopausal anxieties, and the changing roles of women are but a few of the difficulties encountered during this time.

Ruth's story illustrates many common disappointments of this stage. She is a fifty-three-year-old high school teacher with a husband and three children. As a working mother all her adult life, she played the unheralded role of "super-woman," getting her family off to work and school each morning, cooking meals, and keeping the house, while at the same time contending with an often frustrating full-time job.

> How did I do it? I didn't think about it. I worked because I wanted to and we needed the money. But I also wanted a family so I raised my kids the best I could, which was pretty darn good considering the circumstances. When you want something enough you find a way to get it. That's all!

With the children grown up and away on their own, however, Ruth's life has not gone as expected. Her husband suffers from heart disease and she has tired of teaching in the racially torn school system in which she has worked for over twenty-five years.

> I thought that when I reached fifty, my life would get easier. The problem of juggling two careers would be solved when my kids left home. I expected that Sol and I would be pretty comfortable financially, and so on. But with the economy in such a shambles and Sol's illness, we don't have the money for a leisurely way of life. I'm still working too hard and getting too little back for a woman of my age. At this point, I had hoped to enjoy the fruits of my efforts.

Ruth's complaint is common. In later middle age, we expect to reap the harvest of our labor. We want an easing of career pressures and the stresses of raising a family. We hope to put our lives on automatic pilot some of the time and live more comfortably with greater affluence. This is the period when men buy the larger car, when women choose the fur coat. It's a time when we say to ourselves, "If I don't enjoy my life now, I never will!"

Yet with the cost of living rising at a terrifying rate, social security threatened, and pensions drying up, our expectations are uncertain. As Ruth says: "I can't keep going like I did before. Even spring chickens get old. When you're at my stage of life, you don't want to slow down—you *need* to."

Contemporary disappointment in this life phase is not only focused on economic issues. At work, younger employees may be getting the promotions. The fifty-five-year-old executive, vulnerable to the phenomenon of "career plateau," has to contend with the possibility of no further advancement. The elevator to the top has stalled permanently and prematurely. At home, the devoted mother must deal with the loss of her maternal role. As her children establish autonomous lives, she is left without the function and purpose that occupied her for so many years. Now she must pick herself up and find new meaning in life at a time when she has less energy and inclination to make significant change.

As the world changes in response to technological advances and the nature of everyday life is affected, the individual in later middle age may look at the surrounding landscape and see nothing familiar. Libraries without card catalogues, cars that talk back, turntables that can be programmed to pass over an unwanted song—all these are fascinating, but may leave one longing for the accustomed conventions of the past. "Why can't the world be more like it used to be?" is the lament of later middle age. It reflects disappointment in the current condition of things. The longing for the familiarity of the "good ole days" seems to increase with age.

Later Adulthood (65 years and over)

We are a nation obsessed with youth, fearful of death, and either indifferent or callous in our attitude toward older citizens. It is only in recent years that we have begun to address the varied problems of the elderly. Many of these have social origins. In Japan, a country in which the nuclear family remains intact and the aged are revered and sought out for their wisdom, the difficulties associated with the last years of life are absent. The devaluation of America's senior population presents not only a moral dilemma but a practical one as well. A precious natural resource is squandered by our failure to utilize the skills and experience of what T.S. Eliot called our "quiet-voiced elders."

Later adulthood is a period in which the individual wrestles with the issues of integrity and despair. Social attitudes affect this struggle. Will the remainder of life be lived with acceptance of what has transpired and what is fatefully to come, or will it be lived with regret, sadness, and despondency? Will the individual accept "one's one-and-only life cycle as something that had to be and that, by necessity, permitted of no substitutions," as Erikson puts it, or will that person sink into remorse and cynicism, both symptoms of a fear of death?

The elderly must contend with aloneness, the dwindling of physical abilities, illness, the death of friends, and, most importantly, the loss of hope. For the final act contains no encores. Life has run its course. There will be no more surprises. It will never get better. Individuals who concede these realities and still maintain an appreciation of their individual journey, an acceptance of the limits of life, its celebrations and disappointments, and a recognition of its wonder do not fear death. They acknowledge it as the final stage of living.

The disappointments of old age are all connected to an unwillingness to accept death. In one way or another they are statements decrying the loss of future. Here are three to consider:

1. I will not be remembered.
2. I haven't done all that I wanted!
3. Is that all there is?

The failure to leave one's mark on the world—to be forgotten—is the oldest of fears. It is based not only on a desire to maintain some measure of immortality, but on the belief that one's life cannot have had significance if it failed to make an impact on the world. Similarly, frustration over one's level of accomplishment is related to a dread of personal inconsequence. This concern is fed by present circumstance, for the elderly doubt their ability to contribute to contemporary life.

These disappointments protest the failure of particular expectations for meaning and significance, but more than this, they lament the end of expecting itself. For many, the infamous question, "Is that all there is?" is a bit like the one-liner, "The food is terrible, and such small portions!" Regardless of its drawbacks, we want more of life, another chance to make it meet our expectations.

From the vantage point of old age looking back at the roads not taken, the opportunities missed, the failures of nerve, the chance losses, it is easy to focus on what might have been and to live with regret. The danger of this passage is that we will be overwhelmed with the unfairness, difficulties, and pain of existence; that we will bemoan our fate and howl to the gods as we selectively remember the events of our personal histories. Bitterness and disappointment fill the halls of nursing homes everywhere. It is difficult to find justification and meaning in life. Even those who have lived within the boundaries of established religion are hard-pressed to explain senseless injustice and prejudice.

Yet it is in this later period that the disappointed condition takes on the clarity of a full moon on a pitch-black night. With no second chances, there is little point in holding out for the wishes and expectations that can never be. There is only a single path out of regret: to accept life for what it is and what it has been, regardless of whether it falls short of one's dreams. With this understanding comes relief and joy. It is such a simple idea, yet so difficult to put into practice.

CHAPTER 5

Socially Induced Disappointments

In America, an hour is forty minutes.
German Proverb

They are not men, they are not women, they are Americans.
Pablo Picasso

America was conceived and born on a bed of wishes: for the elimination of a class society, for equal opportunity and justice regardless of race or religion, for tolerance and acceptance of all peoples, for prosperity and abundance for those who work hard. Such were the aspirations and hopes of a new country serving as a beacon to the class-oppressed and bloodstained nations of Europe.

Americans, with their legacy of natural resources, manifest destiny, and free industrial expansion, have always believed in the dream of endless possibility. We have been taught to expect more, desire more, imagine more. It is the American Way. Bigger cars, bigger houses, bigger dreams. The sky's the limit! America's hidden purpose has been to prove to the rest of the world that history extends only from yesterday to yesterday. The present and future are boundless. Horatio Alger—the honest, hard-working boy who rose from poverty to riches—epitomized the American myth. Success is promised to anyone who is willing to earn it. And for many these dreams have become a reality. Since 1890, every generation has done better than the one preceding it.

But what happens when the ideals and myths are not achievable? What does a nation experience when its expectations of abundance are dashed? We are entering into a period when endless prosperity is no longer assured. The energy crisis, inflation, high interest rates, soaring levels of unemployment, and the inaccessibility of home ownership make the eighties a difficult period in which to live. Upward mobility may still exist, but the rate is leveling off. With it comes disappointment and a sense of having been cheated. Someone has maimed the dream. Examples: A married couple whose combined income is 66,000 dollars pays about forty percent of it in taxes. The same couple earning an equivalent amount in 1966 (22,000 dollars) paid only twenty-seven percent in taxes. The disadvantage of today's bigger incomes is that they place you in a higher tax bracket, which means you get to keep a smaller percentage of earnings.

According to Harvard economist Richard Freeman, a newly employed college graduate with a liberal arts degree is actually earning thirty to thirty-five percent less in real income than one starting out in 1970. Although the first salary figure might appear substantial, inflation has cut heavily into buying power.

The Boom Generation

Clearly, economic realities are changing. The phrases "downward mobility" and "*nouveau pauvre*" have worked their way into popular usage. Expectations are being readjusted to meet the current situation. But no group seems to have felt the downtrend more than the Baby Boom Generation, that oversized cohort of Americans born between 1946 and 1964. This army of young people represents one third of the country's population, or 76 million Americans. Born into greater abundance and wealth than any group before it, postwar babies were raised on Pablum and promise. No other generation has been the object of so much attention and concern, and none has been its equal in terms of privilege and advantage.

Consumerism was a way of life to the children of this generation. And their parents—believing that gratification was a reflection of love—gave freely. They wanted their offspring to enjoy the fruits of the American dream. This phenomenon was not simply an update of Horatio Alger but an entirely different ethic. Abundance was a given, not something to be earned. It was a birthright.

Freud and Dr. Spock also made an inadvertent contribution to this sense of entitlement. Because he advocated more flexible feeding procedures, Spock was misread as an advocate of total gratification of the child. Freud's deterministic and essentially pessimistic view of human nature was all but ignored. Instead, the implied notion that frustration and conflict were bad for the child reached the public ear. More than any before it, the family of the fifties was child-centered. What was good for one's children was paramount. All manner of sacrifices were made so that Randy could take music lessons, go to ballet class, and attend summer camp. The prevailing ethos was that children should not be denied. Children were the future. Children were the reason for being.

Three important converging forces influenced the Boom Generation and shaped its character:

1. Because of its sheer size, society was forced to make numerous accommodations to it, rather than the other way around. Robert Cook, past president of the Population Reference Bureau, describes the situation this way: "Wherever these children have gone, from kindergarten to college, into massive developments of three- and four-bedroom houses, into the labor market, their progress has caused a shaking of heads over crowding, split school sessions, bulldozing of green acres and job openings." This peculiarity of size gave the cohort, however unconsciously, a false sense of its own power and influence.

2. As the level of affluence in the nation increased and "liberal" childrearing methods replaced more austere and rule-bound traditions, good parenting became synonymous with gratification and the elimination of frustration. Concerned parents wanted to give their offspring all the advantages they never had. Material gratification and caring were linked in the public mind.

3. The social optimism associated with the first healthy economy since the Depression and the emergence of America after World War Two as the world's most powerful nation created a spirit of high expectation that filtered down to the family. Upward mobility has always existed in the culture, but at no other time was the possibility of economic self-improvement so bright for so many. With this renewed vision of the future, postwar babies were delivered this message by their parents: "There are no limits on tomorrow. Anything is possible. We expect you to achieve in ways impossible for us to have contemplated!"

In combination, these three forces produced a generation more privileged, better educated, clothed, fed, and cared for than any other. Advantage, however, carries its own hidden costs. Along with it came a sense of false self-importance, feelings of specialness and entitlement, and a general level of self-absorption that has interfered with interpersonal relations. As writer Fran Shumer points out, "The two burdens parents in the fifties laid upon their children were great expectations and the kind of childhood upon which it is almost impossible to improve."

The Rise of Narcissism

Many social observers, including historian Christopher Lasch, have argued that we live in an era of narcissism distinguished by fear of intimacy, pseudo self-insight, loss of historical time, and self-absorption. Lasch's convincing characterization of American society fits the Boom Generation particularly well. Combine material advantage and the excesses of the child-centered family and you have the soil in which narcissism grows best. Whether the peculiar experiences of this group created the upsurge in self-absorption or simply reflect a response to a larger trend is not clear. Lasch contends that the increase in narcissism represents a realistic way to cope with the tensions and anxieties of modern life. Social critic Hans Morgenthau, on the other hand, asserts its expansion is a response to the failure of religion, science, and nationalism to deal with the universal problem of alienation. Whatever the reason for its rise, there is no doubt of its magnitude, and that the Boom Generation is well suited to the current climate. After all, its credo for more than a decade was "Do your own thing!"

Exaltation of the self is in the air. Devotion to the transformation of the body, diet books, exercise classes, plastic surgery, magazines with egoistic titles like *Us* and *Self*, armies of young people plugged into the impenetrable universe of their own headphones—all are indications that the preoccupation with "me" has never been more pervasive. There have been other periods in history when the celebration of self has taken precedence. The Renaissance, for example, was such a time. But never before has "self" been the preeminent value.

Psychology has reflected this new interest with not only the emergence of "self-fulfillment" therapies but also the resurgence of more traditional "ego" approaches with their focus on "object relations" and separation-independence issues. The term "pathological narcissist" is bandied about with the same joy these days as "conversion hysteria" was in Freud's time. The *Diagnostic and Statistical Manual of Mental Disorders III*, the official source of psychiatric nomenclature, lists the main characteristics of narcissism as: grandiose sense of self-importance or uniqueness; preoccupation with fantasies of unlimited success, power, brilliance; the need for constant attention and admiration; feelings of entitlement; interpersonal exploitativeness; lack of empathy indicated in the inability to recognize how others feel.

In the case of the Boom Generation, doting parents and high expectations joined with social forces to produce an adult population which expected uninterrupted gratification. As one member, a twenty-nine-year-old social service administrator, put it, "I have a sense that I'm entitled. My mother devoted herself to making me feel that way, and she certainly succeeded."

Narcissism as a cultural phenomenon is so commonplace that we scarcely notice it. Like the telephone poles and power lines, it has faded into the background. No one bats an eye when a friend extols the virtues of *Looking Out for Number One, Winning Through Intimidation, Being One's Own Best Friend.* These are not just book titles, they are the clichés of the era. The American ideal of rugged individualism has been replaced by the apotheosis of self. We live in a "me first" society which is marked by a decline of interest in the public sphere and social responsibility. Individuals with narcissistic traits are too engrossed in themselves to make the crossover to another's experience. The other person is merely an audience, an admirer to be used and discarded after the applause has subsided. Human relations are seen as purely utilitarian arrangements: "I use you. You use me. Everyone's happy." Succeeding by any means, regardless of consequence to others, is easily justifiable under these rules. "People will fend for themselves" is the rationalization used to excuse ruthlessness. At the same time, narcissists are particularly vulnerable to criticism. Their overevaluation of self does not allow them to perceive any frailty in their own persons, and they often react to emotional injury with surprise, anger, and depression. It is as if the very foundation on which they base their self-esteem has been rocked.

In the broadest sense, narcissistic traits are necessary for survival. The energy to meet biological and social needs is drawn from self-interest. We could not defend ourselves against aggression, struggle to put food on the table, or fight for our inalienable rights without some measure of self-consideration. The problem, of course, is one of degree.

Narcissism and Disappointment: An Eternal Partnership

The price we pay for self-gratification is high. Aside from the loss of human community and the excessive level of personal exploitiveness, we are caught in two other traps. Although we place great value on self-determination, we are as individuals more dependent on the society for our basic needs than ever before. The energy companies, supermarkets, and clothing-store chains provide our essential goods and services. Our destinies are shaped by the larger forces of international trade and political advantage. Self-sufficiency is largely an ideal of the past. We may exalt the importance of personal freedom, yet we are physically more dependent than at any other time in American history.

Narcissism, as a cultural phenomenon, may be suited to boom times when economic growth and ego expansion can move in tandem. However, if the economy is on the downslide and showing signs of "permanent" exhaustion, as it is now, narcissism inevitably produces disappointment. The Boom Generation, conditioned to high expectations and feelings of specialness, has been the first to feel it.

A young associate professor at Columbia University complains:

I feel like I'm running up against limits, frozen out of things. It may not actually have been that way, but as a kid I felt we were totally financially secure, that there was a lot of money and that if you wanted something it could be had. I never once heard, "Gee, I really can't afford to do this." The first time I heard it was when I said it.

A thirty-one-year-old airline manager reports:

I feel I was born too late. Ten years earlier, people were getting promotions right away and rent-controlled apartments. I've been out of business school five years now, and I'm not living any better than I did when I was a student.

But the problem is not just in the realm of economics. There is a direct relationship between narcissism and disappointment. Self-absorbed individuals tend to overestimate themselves or anything identified with them, like their car, job, or children. They function under the simple formula: What's mine is good; what's yours is less good. From this distortion comes another. Because they see themselves as more valuable, they are entitled to special treatment by others. They expect attention, love, validation, privilege, and respect without having to earn them. This attitude carries over into their relationship with life, which they view as owing them something. Consequently, they believe their existence should be effortless and without frustration, and they resent any compromise of this desire. In the narcissistic view of things, the world revolves around "me." Gratification is a right. Disappointment is not permitted.

Of course, when the privileges of fifteenth-century royalty are claimed by large numbers of people in the twentieth, some sparks are bound to fly. Narcissistic expectations are completely ungrounded in reality. We know that when expectation is faulty, the result is chronic disappointment. Such is the case with narcissistic individuals. They are always disillusioned because their expectations for themselves and life are too grand, special, and unique.

The exaltation of the self has helped to create an altogether unrealistic perspective on what being alive entitles us to have, want, or be. With all its conflict, tension, and anxiety, modern living can never measure up to self-aggrandizing expectations. Cultural disappointment is the underside of cultural narcissism.

Shelley's fateful poem "Ozymandias" reminds us of the perils of self-glorification:

> *I met a traveller from an antique land*
> *Who said: Two vast and trunkless legs of stone*
> *Stand in the desert....Near them, on the sand,*
> *Half sunk, a shattered visage lies, whose frown,*
> *And wrinkled lip, and sneer of cold command,*
> *Tell that its sculptor well those passions read*
> *Which yet survive, stamped on these lifeless things,*
> *The hand that mocked them, and the heart that fed:*
> *And on the pedestal these words appear:*
> *"My name is Ozymandias, king of kings:*
> *Look on my works, ye Mighty, and despair!"*
> *Nothing beside remains. Round the decay*
> *Of that colossal wreck, boundless and bare*
> *The lone and level sands stretch far away.*

Life According to Madison Avenue

In your field of vision you see a gull circling with effortless grace, floating on the windstream high above the billowing waves of the sea. Sensuous, bewitching music plays in the background, calling you away from everyday cares and responsibilities. Suddenly you are at poolside where an elegant woman clad in a scanty black two-piece lies seductively waiting. But for what? The blue waters of the pool reflect the summer sunshine on her tawny skin. A man, equally elegant and evenly muscled, appears from the other side of the elongated pool. He dives in without disturbing the water's surface, an underwater missile moving directly toward the woman. The music heightens. There is the suggestion he will surface at any moment between her legs. You are waiting for the denouement. Just as suddenly, the music fades and a deep masculine voice is heard speaking in authoritative tones.

A dream, perhaps? Or a fantasy? No, these images are an advertisement for a popular perfume. Unable to provide scent samples to the television audience, the manufacturer has hired an ad agency to "express" the essence of the fragrance through sight and sound, and thereby interest consumers in the product.

The average TV viewer is subject to dozens of these thirty-second spots each day and countless numbers of other advertisements on buses, trains, taxis, billboards, radio, and in the print media. Thanks to communication experts Marshall McLuhan and Vance Packard, no one doubts the powerful nature of these ubiquitous messages. They can make or break a corporation, sell a political candidate, even foment a revolution. They surround us, hound us, and often astound us, yet their full impact as a social force has never been really measured. We do know that advertising boosts sales. If we see it on TV, we go out and buy it. Is it that simple?

Fundamentally, advertising informs us of available products and services and extols their virtues. It provides us with a haphazard directory of pain remedies, hair dyes, auto manufacturer rebates, light beer. But of course it doesn't stop there. Advertising creates demand. It influences us to want those things for which we had no use until we viewed the ad. As Calvin Coolidge remarked, "Advertising is the method by which the desire is created for better things."

This function is no accident. Mass manufacturing requires consumer interest to sell its wares. Advertising is the tool used to stoke the fire of acquisitive desire.

Most successful television advertisements communicate directly by presenting us with a series of images accompanied by mood-enhancing sound. The words dubbed over these scenes are of secondary importance. Pictures are more powerful agents of meaning. In this ad, we are confronted with a lovely and sensuous poolscape. Maybe you've had a hard day at work or just fought with the kids. The ideal representation of life on the screen is attracting and comforting. It transports you from the repetitive and dull rituals of existence to romantic fantasy. The initial message communicated by these particular images is: "You can have a better life than you have now. Why settle for less when so much is possible?" By presenting ideal representations of existence free of poverty, illness, death, and responsibility, the ad implies our lives are somehow lacking, thus feeding our dissatisfaction.

Simultaneously, certain valued qualities—in this case physical beauty, sexuality, desirability, and intrigue—are associated with the product. The implication is that if we wear the fragrance, we will somehow attain the promised excitement, desire, and so forth. Thus we buy a brand of cigarettes not on the basis of taste or tar and nicotine content but on the attributes ascribed to it. One brand is associated with western machismo and individualism, another with the liberated female, a third with detached "hipness." The product itself is not inherently any of these things. It is advertising that has made it so by presenting two contiguous images in order to associate one with the other. Using this basic principle of psychological conditioning we could conceivably sell dog food on the basis of sex or antifreeze on its relationship to leisure. The second message of advertising is: "Buy this product and the traits ascribed to it will come into your possession." Because we want these esteemed qualities to enhance ourselves, we willingly participate in this strange game.

In a larger sense, advertising is selling not a particular product but consumerism itself as an answer to the human predicament. The third and most inclusive message is: "Yes, existence is filled with loneliness, anxiety, boredom, meaninglessness. The way to avoid these discomforts is to surround yourself with all manner of goods. Acquisition is the answer to alienation and misery."

Taken together, the three messages of advertising create a scenario for disappointment:

1. Ideal representations distort reality and call our attention to what we don't have. We are disappointed because our world doesn't measure up to the "perfect" images that ads present.

2. By associating products with valued attributes, ads create false expectations. When we buy the perfume and fail to acquire the associated qualities, we experience letdown.

3. Consumption does not provide happiness or an answer to the problems inherent in living. We don't reduce our loneliness or anxiety by the purchase of a food processor or a fur coat. By promising a panacea which it cannot deliver, advertising creates false hopes.

Beyond these disappointments, specific advertising themes indirectly create the preconditions for disappointment. Al-

ways successful at exploiting cultural trends, ad executives
have observed the movement toward narcissism in the culture and are now using the issue of entitlement to appeal to
the mass audience in order to sell goods and services. Hence,
we are now inundated with the message "You *deserve* a break
today," "You *deserve* national attention," or "Someday soon
you'll have only the best [implied: you *deserve* it], so why
not start now with..."

Why do we fall for such trickery? There are many explanations: gullibility, wish fulfillment, attraction to a promised
outcome, avoidance of reality, relief from boredom. There
is little doubt, however, that we would not be such easy
prey for the advertising industry if we really knew what we
wanted from life. In an age of continual technological and
social change, when the traditional satisfactions of family and
work achievement have lost their appeal, we are left groping
for meaning and direction. Under these conditions, any snake-
oil peddler with a product and a promise can snare even the
most wary individual. Advertising is the pied piper whom
we willingly follow down the road to disappointment.

Media Myths

We live in the media age. Our view of the world is shaped
by the information we receive and the manner in which we
receive it. Whether by "Dear Abby," the six o'clock news,
an intergalactic space fantasy, or an ad for an overnight delivery service, the media link us to a larger community and
influence our perception of what is real. The fact that the
leader of the most productive nation in the world is a former
media celebrity testifies to the stature and authority of the

communications industry. Today, virtually any person on the street will concede the powerful role it plays in our lives.

When television became a cultural force in the fifties, most social psychologists thought it would have a revolutionary influence. Having observed the startling effects of propaganda during World War Two, they believed TV would make us a nation of homebound, passive drones, living vicariously through the lives of a favorite sitcom or soap hero. As more extensive research was done in the sixties, it became clear that the earliest fears of the social scientists were unfounded. TV and movies were shown, in fact, to have an almost negligible effect on daily living patterns. Subjects ignored messages that ran contrary to existing attitudes and beliefs. The power of the media to influence behavior, studies claimed, had been blown out of proportion.

Sociologist Herbert Gans has labeled these two nascent viewpoints the "hyperdermic" and "selective perception" theories. In the first, the media is seen as freely injecting ideas into an accepting, quiescent public that is essentially gullible and suggestible. In the second, the audience is viewed as discriminating and impervious. It absorbs information that supports its view of the world and discounts contradicting ideas and values. The hyperdermic position assumes a cause-and-effect relationship between violence on television and violence in the culture. The selective-perception theory contends that only aggressive individuals will seek out violent programming and that peaceable viewers will not be influenced by it.

While both opposing perspectives have some validity, the truth is found between them. More sophisticated current studies indicate that frequently, when watching television and movies, we are selective and critical, taking sharp issue with what we see. Other times, like a dry sponge, we mind-lessly absorb the messages that bombard our sense apparati. How we react depends as much on mood, context, and fre-quency of exposure as on the message itself.

If the newer research on behavioral effects is less defin-itive, what can we say about the influence of the media on something as intangible as expectation or desire? We do know that young children, on seeing commercials for toys and games, express strong wishes for the advertised product. We also know that television and motion pictures, which provide both sight and sound, are very effective tools for learning. Virtually anything, from the alphabet to Greek philosophy, can be taught if there is sufficient attention and proper reinforcement. Can there be any doubt that the me-dia influence our level of material desire and serve as an instrument of learning about life? It is only a short step from "Sesame Street" to the electronic university.

Although the media's vision of reality is distorted by the limitations of its technology and the twin requirements to entertain and show a profit, we are surrounded by evidence of its impact on the culture.

Examples: Costumes in a popular movie set a fashion trend that dominates the clothing industry for months; a television series about the painful struggles and triumphs of a black American family catalyzes national interest in genealogy and a new respect for ethnic differences; an interspace adventure with wondrous visual effects influences the content and di-rection of imaginary play for a generation of children. As McLuhan reminds us, the media are extensions of ourselves. They are the functional equivalents of personal experience. Their effects can be immediate or delayed, short or long term, direct or indirect.

Indonesian President Sukarno, quoted in *Variety*, acknowledged the power of film to influence expectation when he declared:

> The motion picture industry has provided a window on the world, and the colonized nations have looked through that window and have seen the things of which they have been deprived. It is perhaps not generally realized that a refrigerator can be a revolutionary symbol—to a people who have no refrigerators. A motor car owned by a worker in one country can be a symbol of revolt to a people deprived of even the necessities of life. . . . [Hollywood] helped to build up the sense of deprivation of man's birthright, and that sense of deprivation has played a large part in the national revolutions of postwar Asia.

What Sukarno knew, and what we in America have not given enough notice, is that the media supply a view of material possibility that is eye-opening. To a man from New Guinea the most memorable scene from a TV series may be the close-up of modern plumbing. In much the same way as advertising, movies and television present us with a cavalcade of desired products and services. We see magnificent houses, landscaped gardens, sailboats, late-model automobiles, appliances of every color and function. In effect, the wide screen is one large free-market commercial. McLuhan agrees:

> When the movies came, the entire pattern of American life went on the screen as a nonstop ad. Whatever any actor or actress wore or used or ate was such an ad as had never been dreamed of. . . . The result was that all ads in magazines and the press had to look like scenes from a movie. They still do.

This material array has the power to produce a sense of insufficiency and acquisitive desire that leads to resentment and disappointment with one's own level of accumulated wealth. Where the gap between what is pictured and what is possessed is largest, the dissatisfaction is most keenly felt. In this way, TV and movies function much like advertising. Instead of associating products with a desired attribute, however, they link them to appealing characters with whom we can identify. When the heroine escapes in her Porsche, tires screaming, the car's image is enhanced, as is the viewer's desire to own one.

Beyond the advertising effect, TV and motion pictures act in other ways to produce disappointment. Hollywood and major networks are big business. They need to produce films and programs that will draw at the box office and rate well on the Nielsen scorecard. To accomplish this goal, they use themes that appeal to the interest and concerns of a mass audience. Universal issues that transcend class, regional, or cultural barriers are favored. Over the years the media has learned that it is both entertaining and profitable to exploit the rich arena of American myth—those popular collective beliefs based more on how we wish the world to be than the way it really is. Earlier I spoke of these desires as profound lifewishes for glamour, excitement, fairness, romance, love, safety, freedom, and so forth.

A blockbuster film about the uphill battle of a club fighter gave birth to two sequels because it appealed to our wish for the victory of the underdog against great odds. At last, the wide screen delivered what the real world would not: justice and a happy ending. Soap operas have moved into prime-time television slots because they are emotional tarpits supplying vicarious interpersonal excitement. They offer an amplified slice of life, exorbitant and overstated but satisfying in its appeal to our wish for drama and the destruction of the archvillain. Even the westerns—masquerading in their current form as cop shows—have been a mainstay of both TV and movies because they create the perfect context for a morality play. They indulge our wish for a benevolent father who wins out over the forces of anarchy and chaos.

In perpetuating these myths, the media pamper our illusions and distort our world view. Of course, some of what we ingest will be spit out as fraudulent or pure fantasy in accordance with the "selective perception" hypothesis. But a great deal more will sink into the holding tank of the unconscious. Given the number of hours Americans spend in front of the "tube" and the ever-increasing attendance records at local cinemas, this seepage is inevitable. To paraphrase a modern adage, "You are what you watch."

It's not that Hollywood and the networks implant illusions and myths in our collective psyche. They simply play to the already existing wishful notions acquired in childhood. The dangers are obvious. Life can never match the wide screen for romance and drama. If in our daily living we expect "to live happily ever after" or "see the bad guy get his just deserts," we can almost count on feeling disappointed. The pseudo-reality of the media gratifies our wishes and distorts our sense of possibility.

One of my patients, a generally cautious twenty-nine-year-old civil engineer, commented on the connection between his unsuccessful relationship and the movies:

I don't know why, but I expected her to be flawless, larger than life. And I thought we were playing out a great drama like you see in the movies. Boy meets girl. They fall in love and, in spite of the odds, overcome the impossible. They do what everyone else says can't be done.

But it didn't happen. When I look back I see that even after the first week there were problems. I just didn't want to face them. I wanted it to be like a Hollywood story. Reality just caught up with us.

Aside from exploiting our lifewishes, the media influence expectation in more subtle ways. Have you ever noticed that on the screen the hero never shines his shoes or flosses his teeth? Neither does the heroine hem a skirt or return spoiled merchandise to the supermarket. The commonplace events of modern life so necessary for survival are rarely shown on film except in the *cinema vérité* or as a backdrop to make a point about loneliness or boredom. Life is portrayed in highlights without the duller moments that make up most of experience.

Let us say, for example, that we see a film about a boy and his dog. We leave the theater feeling unaffected. The theme is too sentimental and trite; the myths on which the story revolves too mawkish. At the same time that we are consciously repudiating the film's influence, we are viewing a drama that has a beginning, middle, and end; that builds to a climax and finds resolution; that is observed from the outside by an omniscient observer. The structure of the film—if not the content—affects our view of reality.

Daily living does not follow such a neat course. It is often difficult to recognize a beginning amid the myriad of events that transpire at any given time. Endings too are frequently overlooked. Only the ritualized demarcations, sadly lacking in spontaneity, receive attention (weddings, funerals, and so forth). Likewise, the dramatic denouement so necessary to the unraveling of the plot is missing in real life. There is rarely an evenly developed crescendo of events which clearly resolves itself. Real life is messy, unpredictable, and sometimes problems drag on interminably without solution or closure.

Art imitates life, but it is also a fact in this media age that the reverse is true. We mimic our art forms and distort reality in doing so. Film and television present a vision of possibility that is perfect—observable, dramatic, faultless. Real life, on the other hand, although at times dramatic, is generally mundane, flawed, and ambiguous. Events proceed without the control of an accomplished director. There are no retakes, no editing, and no easy moral lessons. The media beckon us to see the world in their particular way. By expecting our lives to mirror the clarity, order, and histrionics of television and motion pictures, we create the preconditions for disappointment. Our challenge is to maintain sensible expectations in the face of exorbitancy.

The Promise of the Weekend Guru

In the last decade, interest in psychology has flourished as greater numbers of individuals seek help in dealing with the problems of modern life. Burgeoning new professional schools have sprung up all over the country, and universities are swamped with requests for more psychology courses. Magazine racks loaded with advice from friendly professionals and self-help books of every persuasion litter the supermarket checkout lines. Weekend seminars at three hundred dollars a shot promise to change your life in just forty-eight hours. Turn on the radio and you'll hear an empathic young Freud doing an abbreviated counseling session live on the airways. Even current language is filled with the jargon of the trade. At the most innocent of cocktail parties you may overhear someone talking about a "psychosomatic reaction," a "neurotic addiction," or a friend with "anorexia nervosa."

Psychology is no longer the exclusive province of a few highly trained academicians or compulsive, depressed analysts. It has gone public. Everyone has a piece of it—from the local clergy to the oil company executive. The hunger for psychological solutions to the problems unanswered by religion, family, and the schools runs deep, but it has not always been this way.

Popular psychology has traded on the credibility of science and a widespread cultural acquiescence to "experts" in order to gain acceptability and influence. Sometimes it fails to keep the public trust by offering shoddy service and pledging improbable results. It always walks a thin line between the demands of a responsible profession and the temptation to exploit public interest and ignorance for personal gain. Phony cures and exaggerated claims can draw big bucks. And it is often only a matter of opinion as to whether a new technique is effective or a cheap and empty hoax.

In attempting to address the problems of daily living, the revolution in popular psychology has created a new dilemma for the public. Below are a series of advertisements which give some sense of the problem:

> Now I don't think about myself, I *am* myself. . . . Things I wanted to do and have were vague dreams in the future before—now they're my life around me.
>
> Book Advertisement

> An easy-to-learn system for literally *tripling* your self-confidence.
>
> Seminar and Materials
Advertisement

> If you are like most people you are probably frustrated, unfulfilled, lack energy, don't have real love and you never get exactly

what you want in your life.... Are you ready to dramatically change all this?... Your life will be an experience of splendor and peace.

Pamphlet Advertisement

Lose weight, relieve stress, gain health, confidence, discover new talents, improve memory power, develop a dynamic winning personality.

Book Advertisement

Does anyone believe these claims for tripling self-confidence, attaining perfection, finding splendor and peace? Unfortunately, people in pain, willing to take grave risks for any possibility of relief, are the natural targets of this hype. Like any good salesperson, popular psychology hawks its wares by accentuating the positive and ignoring the negative. It implies, fore example, that an easy and rapid metamorphosis to a happier, more satisfied life is possible for everyone. Such an implication produces unrealistic expectations— frequently unmet—about the nature of change as well as the limitations of a given technique or therapy.

We can observe three mistaken notions fostered by pop psychology which are directly correlated to disappointment. *Instant Change:* We are a nation that thrives on the instantaneous, or what psychologist Robert Kriegal calls the "McDonald's Syndrome." We drink instant coffee, eat instant vegetables, and cook instantly in microwave ovens. We require instant printing, instant automated bank tellers, instant satisfaction. Is it any wonder we now have instant psychological cures? In one or two weekends, we are promised a new outlook on life.

An auto parts manager had this to say about his weekend enlightenment seminar:

At first I was apprehensive. I was intimidated by how convinced the facilitator seemed to be and I had trouble connecting with the unfamiliar phrases he used over and over again. After a while I settled into it. For that much money I figured I better pay attention. Then, after a few people around me started to get very emotional, I sort of let myself be open to it, and sure enough I started feeling convinced that what this guy was saying was right. I *was* the author of my own experience. I held control over my life. I felt great. The whole world made new sense to me. I walked out of there like a car with a fresh coat of paint. For the next week or so I strutted around on a cloud.

Gradually, though, what I learned began to fade. It wasn't that I forgot the message so much as that it didn't seem to carry the same weight. I could remember the facilitator's words, but they didn't inspire me anymore. Soon it was just the same old me. It was a good experience, but it didn't stay with me.

The weekend enlightenment experience is similar to the LSD trip so popular in the last decade. The drug opened people's eyes to new possibilities, but it did not accomplish the change needed to reach the larger vision. That process is a long journey that involves greater sacrifice and effort. Substantive change demands awareness, motivation, decision, action, and time. The promise of the weekend guru in the long run creates more disappointment than can be justified by what it does provide.

Change without Pain: A favorite myth of faddish psychology is that change can occur without pain or setback. The assumption is that a new set of functional behaviors or attitudes can be superimposed on the old without giving up anything. This way of thinking fails to consider the power and benefit of neurotic behavior. Individuals don't hold onto their dysfunctional attitudes simply out of habit. They keep them because they serve a perceived function. Neurotic persons believe they need to maintain their self-defeating patterns in order to allay the dread of greater terrors or anxieties. Thus an individual may retain a phobic reaction to crowds which prevents her from carrying on a normal worklife in order to avoid a greater underlying fear of failure.

With this in mind, we can see that every change is threatening because it requires surrendering something that is viewed as vital or familiar. Yet change, by definition, demands that we give up one way of being for another. In doing so, we suffer the pain of dispossession, and to this extent some degree of discomfort accompanies all new behavior. The illusion of painless change creates additional disappointment when the real nature of self-improvement becomes apparent.

Knowledge Produces Change: Another common misconception advanced by the popular psychology revolution is that knowledge alone produces change. Reading a text about anxiety, for example, should help you to reduce your own level of tension. Yet the world is full of educated therapists who themselves have the information but not the readiness to change! Education and insight are helpful in any circumstance, but they cannot produce effect without accompanying motivation and action. We must possess the desire and willingness to experiment with new behaviors and attitudes for any adaptation to take place. How many times have I heard a patient plaintively declare, "I know all about my problem but I can't seem to shake it!"

The process of internal change is rarely a straight line. We don't move from A to B as if climbing a staircase. On the contrary, we may take five steps up and then retreat two. Eventually we get to our desired destination, but not without faltering. The limitation of a single psychological intervention like a weekend seminar or a useful book is that neither provide help when you slide back into old patterns.

The growth of popular psychology has offered a great deal to the consuming public in the way of inspiration, education, insight, and change strategies. But it has also made promises which raise expectations to an inflated level. Disappointment results when we lose sight of the fact that deeper personal change requires time, effort, perseverance, and courage.

When we consider that our attitudes and behavioral patterns are many years old, have been reinforced thousands of times, and serve a function, regardless of how obscure, we can appreciate the inherent difficulties in making change and adjust our expectations accordingly.

CHAPTER 6

Common Disappointments

*If men could regard the events of their lives with more open
minds, they would frequently discover that they did not really
desire the things they failed to obtain.*

André Maurois

Except in times of extreme social upheaval, life is lived on
the most basic personal level. So are most disappointments.
A story, popular several years ago, brings this point home:

> A young newlywed asks his experienced friend how he and his
> wife handle decision-making. "Nothing to it," replies the friend.
> "My wife makes all the minor decisions such as where we live,
> what schools the kids attend, and how much money we spend
> on this and that. I make the major decisions: whether we should
> go to war with Russia, at what level interest rates should be
> set, and who should be appointed to the Supreme Court."

Aside from the implied sex-role humor, the story suggests
that the "life arenas" that really matter are those that cir-
cumscribe our daily lives. People are interested in the larger
picture, yes, but the smaller issues over which they may

exercise some control are paramount. They have immediacy and impact. This is why newspapers are fond of reporting how the man in South Succotash is coping without a job. It sells papers. What is of real human interest is the personal story, because we can identify with its principal characters. We see ourselves in their dilemmas. Our own insecurities are tapped. There, but for fortune... As capable as the human mind is of thinking symbolically, of solving the most complex of abstract philosophical and physical problems, it prefers the comfort of the personal and mundane. The palpable problem draws the attention. We like to think small.

Continuity and Change

What is of critical importance to us these days are the personal subjects widely talked about in popular magazines, therapists' offices, commuter trains, and living rooms of the nation. These are the issues of work, relationship, sexuality, and family. Within these areas we live our lives, expending most of our energy and time. And from each we take some measure of personal validation. Our sense of worth and self-esteem is influenced by our experience in these life arenas. When things are going smoothly, we feel a sense of our own personal value. Feedback is positive: "You're doing fine. You're a worthwhile person. You're fundamentally okay." When there is difficulty in one or more of these areas, our sense of self is undermined. We may doubt our ability to cope and adapt, and our worth as a person may be called into question.

These four arenas, central to our daily and inner lives, are particularly vulnerable to the technological and social changes which have caused an apparent shift in belief and lifestyle in the past two decades. There seems to be no question that we as a nation are moving through a period of value transition. Surprisingly, though, some traditional norms have been curiously enduring, causing what prominent social analyst Daniel Yankelovich calls two simultaneous and opposite trends, one toward continuity, the other toward far-reaching change. The existence of both conventional and new attitudes helps society to maintain its balance while adapting to the requirements of the future. But it also reflects confusion about what we want and expect from life. Yankelovich points to a 1978 opinion poll that is most revealing. Sixty-six percent of respondents agreed that "parents should be free to live their own lives even if it means spending less time with their children"—without question a remarkable indication of a shift in attitude. Nevertheless, an equal number of the same group said they would favor "a return to more traditional standards of family life and responsibility." Such contrasting values side by side are increasingly common. A late-seventies poll revealed that seventy-seven percent of the respondents still thought a woman should put her husband and children ahead of her career, and seventy-six percent disapproved of married men having affairs—evidence of the staying power of certain traditional mores. Yet another recent survey showed that a majority favored both sexes' assumption of responsibility for the care of small children, and only thirty-seven percent condemned premarital sex as morally wrong—signs of coexistent contemporary norms.

Clearly, Americans are caught between the familiarity of childhood beliefs and attitudes and the attraction of new possibilities. We are not certain where we stand, and our expectations and consequently our disappointments reflect this confusion. In a perverse way, our ambivalence about what we want has increased the likelihood of disappointment. Rather than surrender one group of expectations for another, we appear to be holding onto both. In effect, we want it both ways—the security and comfort of established patterns and the freedom to choose more personally fulfilling alternatives. Two sets of expectations at odds with each other must be satisfied.

Our uncertainty has created a secondary problem as well. In relationships of all types, we are puzzled about what is expected from us. Should we play the dutiful breadwinner, the stay-at-home wife, the faithful spouse? Or do we trade these roles in for newer models—the working mother, the single parent, the childrearing father? These questions cause as much personal concern for the middle-aged couple struggling to keep their relationship alive and interesting as for the newlyweds who must encounter the problems of dealing with their partners' expectations for the first time. In the past, when cultural norms showed less variation and we knew precisely what was expected from us in the areas of love, work, and family, the situation was less complex. We must now pay more careful attention to the signposts that identify the hidden agendas of others. The more impermanent and discordant the societal norms, the harder the task becomes.

Relationships

Impermanent and highly perishable, many relationships today hardly move beyond infancy before dissolution. Divorce rates are staggering and continue to climb each year. In 1979, nearly 1.2 million people were divorced, as compared to the 1960 figure of just under 400,000. In 1960 there were thirty-five divorced people for every thousand who were married. By 1979 that figure had tripled to ninety-two people per thousand. And the median duration of all marriages ending in divorce is slightly more than six years. The phenomenal rise in the rate of sexually transmitted diseases also testifies to the huge number of "noncoupled" individuals. Single-person households comprise twenty-three percent of all living arrangements, and this category grew at a rate of sixty-six percent between 1960 and 1980.

With these shifts in lifestyle come predictable and unexpected changes in attitude. A 1978 survey showed that sixty percent of those interviewed believed that most people who get married today do not expect to remain so for the rest of their lives. And another opinion poll taken about the same time revealed a more shocking reshaping of mores. Only twenty-five percent of respondents held condemnatory attitudes toward single lifestyles. Compare this figure with a similar 1957 survey in which eighty percent agreed that for a woman to remain unmarried, she must be "sick," "neurotic," or "immoral."

Despite these more flexible attitudes, or possibly because of them, people seem to complain louder than ever about their intimate relationships. Women object to the failure of men to commit themselves to loving partnerships. Men accuse women of being overly demanding and too intrusive. In the face of these conflicts and aggravations, couple therapists are doing a thriving business. Living in a world that often appears to have gone berserk, with the nuclear sword of Damocles hanging over our heads, we desperately seek the shelter and sanity that a relationship can afford. Yet we don't linger long. When the disappointment builds, we head for the nearest exit. Staying power is in short supply.

Relationship disappointments can be grouped into three categories, those pertaining to: partner (you); functioning of the relationship (us); and the self (me). Knowing in which group most of your disappointments fall can be helpful in understanding more about the nature of your expectations.

Disappointments in Partner

Examples: "He used to be so attractive but he's let himself go"; "He's just not the loving person I expected him to be"; "I thought she was less interested in money and possessions"; "She never changes."

If you find that your disappointments fall exclusively into this group, you must determine if your expectations are excessively high. Must your intimate partner combine social graces, good looks, and high achievement with financial success, piercing intellect, and gentle demeanor? In this time of changing social values, there is a tendency to combine traditional and contemporary expectations, to secure, in effect, the best of both worlds. Many of us want our partners to be lovers, business associates, coparents, therapists, friends, mothers or fathers, playmates, intellect titillators, roommates, companions, as well as husbands and wives. Taken as a whole, such demands produce a heavy burden that few can shoulder.

Honeymoon Expectations: Sheryl met Paul five years ago at a United Nations gala when he won her affection by plucking a flower from the floral decorations and presenting it to her. She had thought it a wonderfully iconoclastic and romantic gesture. Paul's arrival in her life seemed her true destiny. After an extended courtship with midnight walks in the park and vacations in Europe and the Caribbean, they decided to marry. Sheryl felt her deepest dreams had come true. The romance was right out of the pages of *Cosmopolitan* and *Modern Romance*. Yet after a while, things began to sour. She saw that Paul had a mean streak, that he was less interested in her than she had thought, and that he could be dull and rather boring. She felt tricked and trapped. He wasn't the man she had married.

Every relationship has a honeymoon. Not necessarily a vacation, this is a period when anything your lover does is novel, fresh, and therefore exciting. Love is at its blindest. What is happening is that you are projecting highly desirable attributes onto your partner. You want him to be a certain way and so unconsciously you organize your perceptions to support your wishes. At the same time, he is trying hard to put his best foot forward and inhibiting his more objectionable behavior. When the honeymoon is over, when objective fact can no longer be ignored and your partner gets tired of putting on "company behavior," reality surfaces and along with it disappointment.

Sheryl failed to recognize that her initial vision of Paul as the ideal man was a function of the honeymoon experience. Her expectations were overblown and idealized. It was only a matter of time before the balloon burst.

Incongruent Expectations

Idealized expectations are only part of the problem. We may also hold expectations that are quite reasonable in themselves but ill-suited to our partners. Suppose I expect my spouse to join my family and play the role of daughter to my parents. This is a natural expectation which countless numbers of people have met. But suppose my wife has different feelings. Her childhood was traumatic and, try as she may, she feels alienated by the daughter role. My expectation is not unreasonable, but it is incompatible with her sensibilities.

A friend of mine was always disappointed that his wife was a poor athlete and could not join him in a game of tennis or racketball. His expectation was not patently unreasonable. It might have fit another life partner, but it was obviously unsuited to his spouse. By maintaining an incongruent expectation for her, he continually fed his sense of disappointment.

The exit from this dilemma is to develop expectations that are not grossly incompatible with your partner's character or abilities. This position requires that you accept your partner and not try to make him or her over to fit your specifications. If acceptance feels impossible, it may be a clue that you are with the wrong person.

Disappointments in the Functioning of the Relationship

Examples: "We don't pay enough attention to each other"; "I don't feel supported by the relationship"; "The romance is gone"; "We never have fun anymore"; "We don't talk about the relationship enough."

If you discover that most of your disappointments are in this category, you might begin by examining whether your expectations for relationships in general are attainable. Below are three mistaken notions that typically produce disappointment.

Relationship as Panacea

Those who have had limited experience or success with primary relationships frequently hold the expectation that intimacy is the answer to all their problems. They envy people in long-term marriages and explain away their personal problems as a function of their aloneness.

Coupling is a preferred condition for many people, but it is not a panacea. Emotional difficulties plague those in relationships just as doggedly as those who live alone. While some basic needs can be met through intimacy, the drives for autonomy, creativity, and assertion must be gratified in other places as well. In fact, most healthy relationships survive because partners find additional satisfactions outside their shared experience.

Expecting the romantic bond alone to provide a remedy to life's problems is an idealized notion which leaves the naive partner despairing when the relationship fails to measure up to what is anticipated.

Passion Is All It Takes

The mistaken expectation here is that because the couple has a powerful sexual connection, they will have a good relationship. Passionate sex and compatibility are assumed to be one and the same. However, ardent lovers don't necessarily make good lifelong partners. People are often physically aroused by just the sort of person who is ill-suited to them. Witness the appeal of the archetypal "macho man" or the beautiful but mysteriously aloof woman.

The notion that passion is all that is required for a relationship to succeed produces unrealistic expectations and may lead to the sort of frustration expressed by one of my patients: "I don't understand how two people so great together in bed could be so mismatched out of the bedroom!"

Love Is Enough

This faulty expectation is similar to the one above except that love is substituted for passion. The disappointed individual expects that if she just loves her partner enough, the relationship will succeed. He will reciprocate with equal feeling and all her needs will be met.

Because one person loves deeply offers no guarantee that the love will be returned. And even if it is, a successful relationship requires more than mutual feeling. Open and clear communication, a shared reality, physical attraction, and good conflict-management are also required. Love is a foundation on which the rest of the relationship is built, but it does not stand alone.

Nonreciprocal Expectations

If your general expectations for relationships are not unrealistic but you still feel disappointed, the problem may result from what I call nonreciprocal expectations. You and your partner may have a different view of what you want from an intimate bond. For example, Ted complained that

Maureen was not available enough to him and that she put her career before all else. He accused her of selfishness and a fear of commitment. In truth, Maureen simply expected something different from her primary bond than Ted. She saw it as less central to her life, one piece of a larger pie. By contrast, he conceived of it as the primary involvement around which everything else was organized. His disappointment was not the result of a character flaw in Maureen but of differing expectations.

In such circumstances, the most fruitful course of action is to sit down with your partner and identify expectations and disappointments in the functioning of the relationship. Each person must clearly delineate his or her sentiments and acknowledge the other's feelings without defensiveness. No one is wrong in this situation. It is natural for people to differ in their view of things. The real question is what sort of compromises can be made to allow both partners to feel a sense of satisfaction without a loss of integrity. This requires a spirit of goodwill and a willingness to give up something for the sake of the relationship.

Antiquated Expectations

Relationship disappointments sometimes result from one partner operating under a set of old expectations in new circumstances. Greg and Sarah got along quite well until their first child was born. Soon after, Greg began to feel neglected and excluded. In his view of things, Sarah spent an inordinate amount of time with the baby and was ruining both their lives in the process. Although a third person had joined the household, Greg continued to expect Sarah to respond to him in much the same way as before.

Jerry and Peter found themselves in a similar situation when one of them went back to finish school at age thirty-five. The other assumed life would proceed as usual. Expectations were not adjusted to fit new realities and the resulting friction nearly toppled the ten-year relationship.

When people or circumstances change, our attitudes must also shift to accommodate. When they do not, disappointment and dissatisfaction result, often with dire consequences.

Disappointments in Self

Examples: "I'm not capable of love"; "I can't seem to please her no matter what I do"; "I keep making the same mistakes"; "I never choose the best person for me."

If most of your disappointments fall into this category, you are likely the kind of person who tends toward self-blame. As a matter of course, such individuals immediately assume that if a problem exists—no matter what the life arena—it must be due to their own shortcomings. Thus if your spouse is dissatisfied, it is a reflection of your inability to please. Or if your lover is angry, it must be because you did something wrong. Self-blamers are overfocused on their own inadequacies and not focused enough on the interactional patterns which are the problem in a majority of relationships. Their aggressive impulses are stifled and they feel as if they have no right to assert their points of view or preferences. Their anger is turned back against themselves, frequently taking the form of disappointment in their behavior or performance.

Of course, most of us are disappointed in ourselves at some time. We don't always act with altruism or grace. Occasional disappointment in self may be a motivating force to do better the next time or seek needed assistance. Frequent disappointment, however, is self-destructive and feeds the individual's feelings of defeat.

Those with a great many disappointments in self must reassess whether they are assuming too much responsibility for failed expectations and begin to recognize the self-defeating nature of their patterns. They must face the fear of provoking the disapproval of others and acknowledge the right to assert for themselves.

One final word about disappointment in relationships. Sometimes it is not what it appears to be. Like most behavior, it can be used as a screen to hide other feelings or actions. Some people, for example, act disappointed when what they're really feeling is anger. They focus on real or imagined unmet expectation as a way to avoid a deeper level of resentment or rage. In effect, they choose a more cautious path to express their emotions. It is safer to be disappointed than to feel anger, betrayal, or abandonment. Others express disillusionment in their partners when they are really disappointed in themselves. Their feelings of letdown are projected onto a convenient target in order to evade a confrontation with their own sense of failure.

Similarly, disappointment can be used as a ploy to indirectly manipulate behavior. The admission "I am disappointed in you" is a charged disclosure, pregnant with suggestion. It is often experienced as "In the future, you'd better shape up." By expressing disappointment, the dissatisfied partner avoids the risk of actually demanding change while the disappointing counterpart may feel threatened or guilty enough to modify behavior. He or she may think, "If I want to keep my partner's love, I'd better make a change," or, "I really let my partner down and should try harder next time." In either situation, disappointment serves as a disingenuous force in shaping behavior.

The Sexual Comedown

In less than half a century, society has undergone a rapid change in sexual attitudes. Formerly taboo activities, such as premarital sexual relations, are generally considered acceptable behavior. Decriminalization of all sexual acts between consenting adults in private settings has occurred in many states. Abortion is now legal. And, of course, the media give daily air time to frank sexual discussion. There are so many handbooks, guides, and encyclopedias of sexuality that one hardly knows which to buy while standing in the "sexuality section" of the local bookstore. As a nation, we have been supplied and resupplied with a wealth of information.

The cultural suppression of sexuality has been seen by many—including Freud—as the root cause of society's problems. Now that many sexual restraints have been lifted, we have been disappointed to find that sex is just another source of gratification and frustration, devoid of the formidable powers we had assumed. Its greater expression has not brought social happiness or eased individual burdens. On the contrary, it has created a new set of difficulties.

The current ubiquity of sex has taken the very life out of it. Sex has become an exploited commodity, corrupted by an aggressive marketplace that has inundated society with beguiling and misleading ideas. The ultimate orgasm, the G spot, the perfect masturbation technique are sexual fictions that boggle the senses and titillate the imagination. Sex has come out of the closet, and our expectations—formerly a private matter—are now defined for us by others. This state of affairs cannot help but set the stage for greater disappointment. Sex is a highly idiosyncratic activity. One person's pleasure is another's pain. Its popularization poses a danger which may ultimately lead us into greater frustration.

As with relationships, we can identify three categories of sexual disappointment: lover (you); sexual interaction (us); self (me).

Disappointments in a Lover

Examples: "He's just not a passionate person"; "He doesn't want sex frequently enough"; "She's too inhibited"; "She only makes love because I ask her to."

A preponderance of sexual disappointments in this group indicates that you have either been choosing incompatible partners or you expect too much from them. A better way to look at the situation is from a systems perspective. Except in extreme cases, most psychologists prefer to conceptualize sexual dissatisfactions as symptoms of a faulty pattern of interaction. By seeing the physical relationship rather than the unresponsive or overzealous paramour as the patient, they place responsibility for making change on both parties. Emphasizing the system of interaction produces a more accurate picture of what is happening. For example, your partner's sexual appetite may have declined substantially and you may

think, "What a disappointing lover she turned out to be."
But perhaps she is responding to an attitude or behavior of
yours. She could be thinking, "I can't stand the way he jumps
into bed and expects me to be ready for love right away.
Why can't he be more considerate of my feelings?" To focus
only on your disappointment is similar to the actions of a
hockey referee who penalizes Blue for hitting Red in the
mouth, but fails to notice that Blue is responding to Red's
bashing. It all depends upon when you begin looking. By
concentrating on the patterns of sexual interaction you eliminate the arbitrary starting point. The problem and the
disappointment are shared. No blame is assigned. It is a no-
fault approach that creates the basic conditions for change.

Look at your own list. See if you can convert any disappointment from Category A to Category B. For example,
"He doesn't want sex frequently enough" might better be
expressed as "Our sexual appetites differ."

Of course, not every disappointment is amenable to this
intervention. It is possible that one's partner's reduced interest in sex is the result of overwork, illness, or other stresses.
But these are generally temporary phenomena. Any problem
will become an interactional difficulty over time, whether it
begins that way or not.

Disappointments in one's partner may also be the result
of idealized expectations. We frail humans are hardly the
sexual athletes portrayed in the more fanciful sex manuals
and romance magazines. On the contrary, we are highly
sensitive to the emotional context in which the sexual experience is cloaked. We can't turn on and off the sexual tap
without regard to our feelings and values. Despite the current media myths which boast of newly discovered erogen-

ous zones, we have difficulty enough enjoying the simple pleasures of the body.

Disappointments in Sexual Interaction

Examples: "Our sex life is too mechanical"; "We don't do enough touching"; "After twenty years, it's 'dullsville'"; "We never really talk about what we want from each other."

If most of your disappointments are found in this category, you need to consider whether nonreciprocal expectations are a problem. Do you and your partner have a similar vision of the sexual experience and its importance to your bond? After ten years of marriage, Phil looked at sex much like a shot of whiskey on a cold night. It was invigorating and pleasurable, a momentary diversion from other activity. His partner, Marie, had other expectations. She envisioned love-making as a prolonged, sensual experience which allowed for the expression of affection and caring. It was the tenderness and physical closeness that excited her. After years of frustration, Marie felt disappointed, Phil resentful.

At the heart of the problem were differing expectations. Had they recognized this fact, they might have developed a shared perspective. When disappointments in the sexual arena are a problem, the first step is to compare notes with your partner on the role, frequency, and nature of the sexual connection. If you cannot bring differing expectations into line through discussion and compromise, more intense intervention such as counseling may be needed.

The second step is to scrutinize your sexual disappointments for unrealistic expectations. Most of these are so deeply embedded in our psyches that it takes a special effort to be aware of them. A few are considered below.

Passion Forever

The most common sexual disappointment seems to be the loss of passion. Any long-term relationship has an inherent difficulty: keeping sex interesting and vital. It is a problem exacerbated by the age in which we live. When new products make "almost new" products obsolete in a matter of months, we become accustomed to rapid change. In fact, we demand it in our consumption of late model cars, updated toasters, and improved television sets. Has this obsession been transferred to the level of our relationships? Do we now require new lovers to replace our worn-out and familiar partners? When the novelty wears off, the passion fades. Having once experienced it in the sexual relationship, we feel disappointed by its absence. The thrill is gone.

This dilemma is similar to the loss of the honeymoon. The flourish of the first months is over and can never be regained. Yet we somehow believed it would live on forever, although we certainly could not expect such a thing from an automobile or a frequently worn sweater. The problem is that we expected the passion to continue of itself without any help on our part. The expectation is unrealistic.

For the sexual relationship to remain vital, caretaking must be done. Action in the form of attention, discussion, and innovation is what is required to energize the sexual bond. Acknowledge the loss of the expectation and the underlying wish (for the passion to remain forever) and move on from there.

No Talking, Please

We are taught early in life that sexual thoughts and feelings are a private matter, not to be mentioned in mixed company and rarely disclosed, if at all. Values in sexual conduct are changing, but many people still find it difficult to speak openly and candidly to their lovers about their sexual preferences and fantasies. They expect (wish) their partners to know what they want without their having to verbalize it, as if such knowledge were acquired intuitively or automatically. "Let's keep the mystery in sex" is the theme behind which they hide their embarrassment of self disclosure.

In the long run, opening a sexual dialogue prevents a great many confusions and apprehensions. When problems exist in the physical relationship, we tend to imagine the worst: "I'm no longer desirable," "I don't know how to please him anymore," and so forth. Frank discussion clarifies, limits distortion, and provides a sense of control. Actually, talking about sex can be a refreshing and bonding experience if it is done in a spirit of goodwill and cooperation. The expectation that a good sexual relationship can develop naturally without open communication is faulty and misleading.

The Orgastic Must

Compared with the rest of the human community, our society is characterized by a marked goal-orientation. That is, we focus on accomplishment and production. The end result of our efforts is what counts, and the final score, the finished product, the fruit of our labor is what we emphasize. In sex, this attitude is expressed in the primacy we give orgasm. Despite the warnings of sex therapists, many believe that the measure of a sexual encounter is whether both partners reach a climax. Some not only expect to achieve this goal each time but require that the experience be simultaneous and exclusively through intercourse. Such expectations place a burden on both lovers and can make sex more work than pleasure. Besides the fact that many women are physiologically unable to have orgasms exclusively through intercourse (sometimes as a result of the particular anatomical fit with their partner), the emphasis on the sexual finale tends to obscure the rest of the experience. It is like sitting through a symphony to hear the last twenty seconds!

The expectation that orgasm will (should) be reached every time and in a particular manner will always produce disappointment when the unrealistic expectation fails. Orgasm is an important part of the sexual experience but it is by no means a requirement of each encounter.

The Sexual Has-Been

No expectation has been more destructive to the physical relationship of older people than the belief that sexual activity ceases after the individual reaches seniority. Sex researchers Masters and Johnson have demonstrated that healthy sexual functioning can continue throughout the life cycle without interruption. It is true that aging does produce some biological changes in sexual response. For the male, erections may take longer to achieve, ejaculation may be less forceful, and the refractory phase (the time needed for restimulation) may lengthen. For the female, lubrication may take longer and the number of contractions during orgasm may decrease, shortening the experience. Other idiosyncratic changes can also occur. But it is important to remember that these differences are relatively minor in the scheme of things and in no way should be construed as sexual failing.

Desire is largely influenced by attitude. If we expect to lose interest we likely will. Given free reign, however, our bodies will continue to give us pleasure long into later adulthood.

Disappointments in the Sexual Self

Examples: "I can't get an erection"; "I reach orgasm too quickly"; "I've lost my sexual appetite"; "I can't have an orgasm with my partner."

In sexual matters, disappointments in self generally follow frustration over a perceived problem or deficiency. Most sexual difficulties produce feelings of doubt and inadequacy which, in turn, reinforce the problem. Disappointment further exacerbates this cycle, making change even harder to accomplish. It is, therefore, a prescription for continued dysfunction.

Most sexual problems are rooted in poor learning. We have been miseducated about our bodies and our relationship to physical pleasure. This is an essentially hopeful point of view because it implies that new learning can overcome most dysfunction. If you are repeatedly let down by your sexual performance, use your feelings to motivate you to talk freely with your partner or to seek professional help and reassurance.

Expectations for self in the sexual arena need to be kept realistic. In fact, the fewer preconceptions we have about lovemaking, the better. Expectations are artificial impositions on this largely spontaneous activity. It is spontaneity—the sense that this moment is neither planned nor predictable—that gives pleasure to sex and makes it a transporting experience.

Nine-to-Five Blues

The headlines tell the story: HARD TIMES FOR A WHILE; KEEPING LABOR LEAN AND HUNGRY; FIRED IS NOT THE END OF THE WORLD. Clearly, the country is in the midst of economic difficulties. Unemployment has reached record highs. How do these lean conditions affect those with jobs? Do people remain in positions they don't like because there are no better opportunities, and they need to keep the weekly paycheck coming in? For many, the monthly accumulation of bills, fed by continuing inflation, has led to a situation best described by one unemployed autoworker: "Jobs? Be glad you have one!" Yet for others, the traditional questions regarding job satisfaction and working conditions are still at issue. The employed continue to complain about the boss's unfairness, the company's insensitivity to individual needs, the lack of promotion opportunities. A comparison of Gallup Polls taken in 1955 and 1980 reflects a marked decline in the number of employees who enjoy their work. The latter survey found a similar drop in the percentage of workers who preferred their jobs to other activities. Enthusiasm for work was lowest among younger workers, a signal that the current attitude is likely to continue into the future. Gerald Sussman, a professor of organizational behavior at Pennsylvania State University, estimates that one quarter of the labor force—24 million people—is dissatisfied with their jobs for one reason or another. Absenteeism, an index of worker dissatisfaction, is so high that employers lose twenty billion dollars a year in productivity and additional labor expenses. That is more money thrown away than the annual budgets of most countries.

As interest in work for its own sake declines and dissatisfaction increases, disappointment on the job also continues to rise. What are the typical work-related disappointments? We can divide them into two groups, those pertaining to the job (task, salaries, promotions), and those pertaining to interaction in the workplace.

Disappointments in the Job

Examples: "I thought I'd have more control over my work"; "I didn't realize the job was so repetitious and dull"; "I expected more raises and promotions"; "The job doesn't challenge me the way I'd like it to."

People are disappointed most in their job tasks and the corollary issues of salary and advancement. But unlike the other life arenas which are under more personal control, work must be seen in a larger context. Occupational disappointments are influenced by two conflicting social trends.

On the one hand, people expect more from their jobs than ever before. On the other, work itself has become more routine and specialized, offering fewer inherent satisfactions. In a recent poll, *Saturday Review* found significant discrepancies between what readers regarded as important in their work and what they actually did on the job. Eighty-four percent said using one's talents was very important, but only forty-six percent believed their jobs provided such opportunity. Sixty-eight percent said job challenge was important, yet only forty-nine percent felt challenged. Sixty-one percent wanted to make a contribution to society through their work; thirty-nine said they could do so. These findings suggest that people expect a great deal more than money from their labor, but they don't often receive it.

Most employees spend one-third of their waking hours on the job and much of their leisure time thinking about work. They look to it as an avenue of self-expression and meaning. Business, however, listens to a different drummer. Social critics have long argued that the division of labor—the breakdown of production into small tasks—has separated workers from the inherent satisfaction of work. Without a sense of their significance in the manufacturing process or the delivery of services, they perform their specialized functions in a kind of industrial vacuum. Isolation from the larger picture and constant, repetitive activity—whether on the assembly line or in the office—produces alienation, boredom, and a poor product. In fact, a University of Michigan study in the late seventies showed that twenty-seven percent of all American workers felt so ashamed of the quality of the product they were producing that they would not want to buy it themselves! When the task loses its meaning, it provides no satisfaction. The paycheck and benefits package replace the work itself as the primary motivation for showing up each day. Workers display their discontent in numerous ways: by arriving late and leaving early, staying off the job for long periods (absenteeism), and celebrating the end of each work-week ("TGIF"). As computers take over many human functions, there is even less control of circumstances in the workplace. A telephone operator graphically describes the situation:

Maybe some people enjoy just getting a paycheck. I like to know my work is well done. But my job isn't to talk to you like a human being anymore. I'm nothing but a machine now. I have the exact phrases I'm allowed to say. They had me on the carpet last week for saying "I'm sorry" once too often because I felt a person needed to hear it. We aren't people anymore. We're machines now. I'm a machine but only until they can find a real one to take my place.

Thus our disappointment is the result of rising expectations and shrinking possibilities. We want more out of our labor than ever before, but the workplace—slow to respond and subject to other masters—offers us less. At its root, this is a problem of nonreciprocal expectations. The employee expects job challenge, opportunity for creative expression, and some control over the job. The employer expects to show a profit, maximize efficiency, and remain competitive in the marketplace. The basic incompatibility of these two sets of expectations is hard to deny despite occasional overlap.

Without underestimating the impact of social forces, we also need to remember that disappointment is a personal issue, and it is on this level that we *can* make an impact. Some occupational disappointments are clearly the end result of faulty expectation. For this reason it is important that we realistically assess what we can expect from our work. If there is little opportunity for creative activity and advancement, for example, we must recognize the situation and adjust our perspective accordingly. We may, in fact, want to look for other employment. Every disappointed worker would be wise to construct a personal job profile in which working conditions, employee interactions, and the intrinsic nature of the work are carefully and unsentimentally as-

sessed. "Is the work interesting?" "Are supervisors supportive or critical?" "How frequently are promotions given and
under what circumstances?" From this physical evaluation
expectations should be drawn. If these are compatible with
one's goals, individual talents, and aptitudes, the job is probably the right one. If they are not, the employee is headed
for an unhappy and disappointing future.

The story of the work experience of a patient of mine
demonstrates how impractical expectations can lead to disappointment. Flora, a wonderfully outspoken thirty-three-
year-old woman, had been a sociology professor in a large
university for three years before deciding to change careers.
In spite of her love of teaching, she found academia stuffy
and removed from the real world. With support from her
family, she decided to begin a new career as a researcher in
a large advertising agency.

Excited about landing the new job, she spent her last
"free" days leisurely wandering through the city's museums.
But each time she focused on the colors and shapes in her
field of vision, she lost her concentration. Her mind was
preoccupied with the future. She saw her career in front of
her—a challenging odyssey of hard work and reward. She
imagined herself moving up through the hierarchy, gaining
recognition, money, and influence. She held the hope that
she would not only be successful but would contribute in
some measure to the level of honesty and humanism in her
new profession.

> I rather naively assumed that in some way—I wasn't sure how—
> I would bring academic honesty and a belief in nonexploitive
> human values to the world of advertising. I knew such a view
> might be unpopular, but I expected that as I acquired authority,
> I would have control over my own projects.

The first three months were confusing and difficult. The transition from the classroom to the office was more than a change of address. Flora encountered all sorts of covert rules and expectations. She was required to be attractive and "feminine," yet productive and tough. She was expected to be efficient and quick-witted, but not too aggressive and threatening. She was told to initiate, but when she pushed her own projects she was criticized for not being enough of a team player. She perceived her margin for error to be impossibly small. She walked a tightrope between acceptable assertion and expected passivity.

Beyond this predicament, Flora was disturbed by the level of competition on the job. Faculty meetings had often been marred by contentious rivalries, but they were nothing compared to what she experienced in the business world. She saw people getting ahead at all costs. Backstabbing was commonplace, and small deceits were a necessity of survival. Alliances were cultivated to gain advantage and relationships were utilitarian arrangements to facilitate moves up the career ladder. Even communication was characterized by a disturbing indirectness, and jargon masking as sophisticated shorthand served to keep things vague.

Despite her previous experience, she felt unprepared for the intensity of competition, the fierce territoriality, and the scramble to the top. Her unhappiness and disappointment reached a critical level after a special project she headed was scrapped because of financial cutbacks. She suspected other motivation, but the indications of her supervisors did not support her intuition.

After sixteen months on the job, Flora's enthusiasm had turned to cynicism and disillusionment. She was plainly disappointed and frustrated in her new career and wondered just what had attracted her to it in the first place. True enough, she had gained the possibility of earning more money than in teaching, but at this point the salaries were roughly equivalent. Her desire for a taste of the real world had been soured by what she saw as the corruption of opportunism in the corporate structure. As for her hope to advance in the hierarchy and introduce humanistic values along the way, she felt this to be a pipe dream with little chance of success. She remarked: "Believing that I would succeed quickly with my values intact was as unrealistic an expectation as remaining a virgin in a brothel!"

After another six months of serious consideration, Flora decided to leave her job. Even after she recognized that her initial expectations were unrealistic, she felt her personal goals and beliefs were simply incompatible with those of the corporate world. Eventually she found work with a nonprofit foundation which conducted socially relevant research. Although she made less money, the job was better suited to her talents and values. To this day she continues to work there.

What can we learn from Flora's dilemma? First, unrealistic expectations for advancement, promotion, the nature of the workplace, and so forth always produce disappointment. Second, when we feel let down, we need to adjust our expectations to the reality around us and decide whether our skills, goals, and sensibilities are, in fact, compatible with our job. In situations when they are not—such as Flora's—the most enlightened action is to find new employment. In other circumstances, when we can live harmoniously in the work environment with rewritten expectations, remaining on the job makes good sense.

Disappointments in Interaction at the Workplace

Examples: "I expected my boss to recognize my good work"; "I thought I'd have more opportunities for promotion"; "The company doesn't care about me"; "I thought there'd be more cooperation among my coworkers."

Disappointments in this category are similar to interactional disappointments in the other life arenas. Consider the first one on our list. The employee's expectation to receive recognition for good work has gone unmet. Does she expect acknowledgment every time she produces? If she does, is her expectation realistic? To find out, she might look at the experiences of other employees. If they're not receiving recognition under similar circumstances, she needs to rethink her expectation. But suppose she doesn't anticipate acknowledgment every time, just once in a while. Again, she must observe the experience of others in order to measure whether her expectation is reasonable. Now the problem gets more complex. She notices that a few get recognition while others do not. What characterizes that fortunate minority? If they're all related to the boss, she'd be wise to take that into account. If they all work on Saturday, she needs to decide if she's willing to do the same. If not, her expectations should reflect her choice.

In every situation, the realism of an expectation must be measured against the context. In forming our expectations, we must assess not only whether they are possible but whether they are possible in a given situation. To make this evaluation, we need to ask:

1. What is the expectation?
2. Has the expectation been met before by me or others?
3. What were the circumstances in the above situation(s)?
4. Are they similar here?
5. How much control do I exercise over factors which influence the success or failure of my expectation?
6. If the expectation has gone unmet in similar circumstances (or I have no information about previous situations), what leads me to think it will be met now?

The answers to these questions will tell us where to place our expectation on the Attainability Continuum (see page 29).

Suppose the employee's boss is a hardnosed, austere individual who doesn't give praise or acknowledgment easily. He has been overheard to say, "You get paid to work hard. That's your job." Knowing this information, the expectation of even infrequent recognition for good work should be placed at about point five on the continuum. It does not appear likely. If, however, the boss has been replaced by someone who believes in positive reinforcement and has a history of praising those who are productive, the expectation would be placed anywhere between points one and three, depending on the employee's willingness to work hard.

As a rule of thumb, any expectation placed at point five or to its right is not a good prospect and should be considered "disappointment-prone." Similarly, any expectation that requires the cooperation of factors outside one's control is a high risk and should be carefully evaluated.

By using the Attainability Continuum, we can measure the likelihood of meeting our expectations and establish a better ratio between wish and probability. It gives us a practical way to evaluate what we expect so that we can readjust our thinking to reflect greater realism. In turn, these adjustments will produce more successful outcomes and therefore fewer disappointments.

Family: Not the Way It Should Be

The high incidence of divorce, the drop in birth rate, and the break-up of extended family systems suggest that the family, as we know it, is undergoing a facelift or, perhaps, even more radical surgery. No one can predict what the twenty-first century will bring, but we do know that the rules that formerly governed our familial lives are no longer applicable. Father as exclusive breadwinner and mother as primary parent and homemaker are images from the past. In a 1979 survey conducted by Yankelovich, Skelly, and White, only one out of five wanted to return to a traditional style of family life. Single-parent and single-person households are no longer uncommon. In fact, together they account for a startling forty percent of all living-units today. With these changes in attitude and behavior come new expectations and more up-to-date disappointments. For the most part, however, traditional complaints continue to predominate.

Disappointments can be grouped into two categories, those involving children and spouse, and those involving interaction in the family system.

Disappointments in Children and Spouse

Examples: "My children never show any gratitude"; "My son turned out to be nothing like me"; "My kids are lazy and irresponsible"; "My daughter never seems to do well at school"; "My husband just isn't a family person."

Disappointment in one's children is as ancient a theme as Cain and Abel and as contemporary as *On Golden Pond*. As parents, we know that expecting our offspring to grow into world-renowned physicists or major-league ballplayers is most often psychologically damaging, yet the temptation is difficult to resist. Successful children are a source of pride and enjoyment; surely we cannot be condemned for such human desires. But excessive expectations can cripple a child and create enough anxiety and self-doubt to produce defeat and a sense of personal inadequacy. We are all familiar with the "reactive" offspring who becomes a rock-singer rather than travel his parents' preferred route to medical school. The decade of the sixties produced numerous stories of disappointed parents lamenting, "Can't he get a real job instead of playing around with that guitar?"

Why do parents invest heavily in expectations involving their children? First, the child's appearance, behavior, and character reflect on the parents. A beautiful or precocious child enhances the parents' own value and increases self-esteem. Take the case of one of my patients who recalled that his mother forced him to play the piano each time guests arrived. While she basked in the usual shower of praise, he felt embarrassed. He resented these near-weekly recitals, but complied in order to please her. Later on, he gave up the piano. He had associated playing it with parental expectations and unpleasant memories of compliance. Whether intentional or unconscious, placing expectations on your child as a means of manipulating behavior to reflect well on you will likely produce a reservoir of resentment. It may also create disappointment in self as the child struggles to measure up to expectations that are superimposed on him.

Second, parents with excessive expectations may be living vicariously through their children. The child's success is experienced as their own—an antidote to their dissatisfaction and boredom. In this kind of situation, the boundaries between parent and child are unclear, very often to the child's detriment. She may be confused about what she wants independent of those hovering around her. We frequently see such vicarious living in the parents of children engaged in athletic competition. The offspring participates to please the mother or father, who justify their actions by emphasizing the child's intrinsic desire to compete. The parents defend their behavior by pointing to the success of major athletes who were pushed by like-minded mentors. The truth is that the child superstar is rare; the price paid by the average young athlete in psychological and physical terms is very real.

Third, parents expect too much from their children when they perceive them as smaller or younger versions of themselves. This egoistic pattern is naturally reinforced by friends and family members who comment, "Tommy looks just like his mother," or, "She's got the brains of her dad." Identification with one's child can be healthy up to a point. Beyond it, the child's freedom to make decisions and develop a sense of autonomy is sacrificed. Parents may rationalize their behavior behind the self-serving smokescreen: "I know what's best for my child. I've been through it already." Indeed, this statement may be true, but allowing one's offspring to make independent choices for better or worse encourages psychological maturity and teaches the child how to avoid future mistakes.

In the end, rearing children successfully is a matter of balance. Any behavior, regardless of how positive, produces problems when taken to the extreme. Expecting too much from children because of overidentification, boredom with one's own life, or need for esteem produces the scenario for disappointment. When we expect too much too often, we compromise our effectiveness as parents and threaten the well-being of our children.

Disappointments in Family Interaction

Examples: "No one in this family seems to care about each other"; "We don't spend enough time together"; "There's too much conflict in the home"; "There's no sense of traditional family loyalty."

As we have done in the other life arenas, it is important to uncover unrealistic notions regarding the nature of family life. The mass media have a role in influencing these perceptions. Since most families put on their best behavior when guests arrive, an inside glimpse of another family is a rare occurrence. All the more reason why the interior views of domestic life that television affords us carry undue influence. Children in particular are susceptible to the vision of life presented by the major networks. Many of us who are now parents cut our teeth on "The Adventures of Ozzie and Harriet," "Leave It to Beaver," "Father Knows Best," and

"My Three Sons." These programs offered us an idealized armchair view of the family, free of hostility, tension, and malevolence. Almost everyone got along, and when they didn't, a benign, understanding parent helped the kids work through their problems. With just the right amount of sentiment and respect for the authority of one's elders, the entire cast lived happily ever after. Do we as parents expect the same from our families? Many other factors have influenced our original, naive images, but these early views of family life created cultural norms that are permanently imprinted on the recesses of our unconscious. They are a first vision of how the world is arranged.

In addressing the question of whether to raise children, even the most sophisticated may be swept along by the tranquil notions of family life first seen on television. When these images are superimposed on the real-life interaction of a modern American family, there is trouble ahead. It is difficult enough to live with the psychological and physical needs of three or four other people. Any parent can tell you that getting everyone to agree on how to spend a Saturday afternoon often requires the mediating skill of a shuttle diplomat. Ozzie and Harriet never had such troubles. In fact, Ozzie, to my recollection, never had to contend with the stress of a job. He was gloriously unemployed. Complicating the picture with unrealistic images from the past can make a hard situation unbearable.

Similarly, if we expect our current family to behave like our family of origin, we are moving in the same disappointing direction. Most of us remember our early life with fondness. This is because we have screened out the traumatic and unseemly events of our personal histories through the process of selective forgetting—the cognitive mechanism that enables us to distort the past by making inaccessible all painful memory. The result is that the past seems wonderful. We long for it, base political ideologies on it, and cherish it by collecting odd and misshapen objects awkwardly called memorabilia. Because we can distort the past, we run the risk of comparing our present with a sentimental vision of history. When we are disappointed in the lethargy of our teenage children, we just may be operating out of unrealistic expectations drawn from inaccurate memories of our experience. After all, laziness is not new to this generation of adolescents.

Raising a family is a tricky business made more difficult by unrealistic expectations. The most common disappointments are focused either on our children or on the disparity between an idealized view of family life and the way it really is. With this in mind, reexamine your own list of disappointments.

CHRONIC
DISAPPOINTMENT STYLES

Disappointment patterns are built into the structure of the psyche. Biological endowments and personal history determine the attitudes, beliefs, and patterns of adaptation that make up a particular personality. These enduring traits, which vary little with time or place, influence the nature of expectation. Whether one maintains romantic, idealized, or impossibly high hopes has as much to do with character as it does with the specifics of each situation. The essential quality of one's disappointment, therefore, must also be affected by personality.

In ordinary life, this relationship is easily observed. A woman is brought up to think her value is determined solely by her level of accomplishment. In order to maintain a sense of worth, she believes she must set rigid, perfectionistic goals for herself. She has to be the best at everything she does, and she applies these requirements to her children, spouse, and friends as well. Her perfectionism gives all her disappointments a singular flavor. She can't understand why others are always letting her down.

Some personalities are more likely to experience disappointment than others. In the following three chapters I present the acquiescent, deprived, and self-important styles. Each is prone to a particular, chronic form of disappointment that reflects the deeper issues of character.

CHAPTER 7

The Acquiescent Style

I am not in this world to live up to your expectations. And
you are not in this world to live up to mine.

Fritz Perls

Eileen is the codirector of a childcare center in the inner
city. She is a small woman, in her early thirties, married for
the last eight years to a physician. People who meet her for
the first time are struck by her reticence. She is shy, with
a round, youthful face that gives her an innocent appearance.
Her eyes in particular draw attention. They seem to say,
"I'll do anything to please but I'm afraid it won't be enough."
She wears loose-fitting clothing which disguises the lines of
her figure and might be better suited to a larger, older
person. Her manner is mildly deferential, consistent with
her view of herself as a cooperative, moral individual.

She never expresses hostility or anger and has often been
described as a "giving" person, well liked by friends and
family. Rarely does she utter an unkind word. On the contrary, she consistently suppresses any negative feelings of
envy, competition, or aggression. In all arenas of her life,

Eileen works hard to do the "right" thing and win the approval of others. At work she puts in long hours to make certain the daycare center runs smoothly. At home she is a dutiful and attentive wife. With her parents and friends she is always more than willing to give of herself and infrequently asks anything in return.

A work experience typifies her character. About a week before the spring open house at the daycare center, the other codirector approached her with a problem. Her parents were coming to town during the busy week, and she had promised to take them traveling around the area. This visit was important to her. Would Eileen mind if she took the week off? Without hesitation or complaint, Eileen agreed, although she recognized with fleeting resentment that she would be left to plan and supervise the open house alone. By the end of the hectic period she was exhausted and had caught a bad cold. She had sacrificed her well-being to help a friend. Yet such action was not uncommon for her. In spite of her fatigue and physical condition, she would do it again.

Curiously, Eileen's selfless actions do not seem to influence the way she feels about herself. Despite her generosity, she invariably experiences feelings of worthlessness and inadequacy. Always dissatisfied with her level of achievement, she sees herself as second best, never quite good enough regardless of how hard she tries. Her self-critical attitude causes her to be persistently disappointed in herself.

Eileen's story illustrates a specific relationship to disappointment which I have called the acquiescent style. Unlike other patterns overloaded with unrealistic expectation of one's choosing, acquiescent individuals are smothered by the expectations of others. The heart of the problem originates with one impossible requirement: to meet all the demands—

real or imagined—of others. It is a Sisyphian task without hope of success. But this does not deter these compliant personalities. They struggle to achieve the impossible, ultimately trading their own well-being for transitory approval. Disappointment in self is common among such individuals. They feel inadequate and undermined because they respond not from their own inner needs but from their desire to please. Even when they succeed, they fail. The process of continually trying to measure up to others' expectations separates them from their own sense of self.

Eileen's psychological past tells us how this sort of pattern emerges. As the younger of two children and the only daughter in a comfortable suburban household, she formed a strong and early bond with her mother, whom she described as "a housewife with few interests other than her family." Her mother was intimately involved in the daily regimen of Eileen's life. She drove her to ballet class, singing lessons, and to friends' houses after school. From age six, her mother regularly visited her bedroom in the evening to talk with her. Eileen shared her deepest feelings about herself, school, and friends. Mother confided her feelings of loneliness and doubts about her troubled relationship with her husband, who was rarely at home. Eileen had mixed feelings about these nightly talks. She enjoyed her special role as confidante but sometimes felt burdened by the responsibility. There were uncomfortable moments when she wanted to exclude her mother from parts of her life, but didn't, to avoid hurting her.

Mother selected Eileen's clothing, helped her with her homework, guided her friendships, directed her relationships with boys, and counseled her about the future. She was interested in every facet of her daughter's life and encouraged her with praise whenever she lived up to her standards.

> It's strange, but unlike my friends I never fought with my mother. I always assumed she was acting in my best interest. Fighting with her always made me feel wrong somehow. I remember one time she didn't like a friend I had made at school. I recall how strange I felt about ignoring this person but I knew I'd feel guilty if I didn't. I broke off the friendship just like that. I felt I couldn't afford to lose my mother. She was my best friend.

Eileen's father, an orthopedic surgeon, was rarely at home. During her childhood their relationship was tenuous, and she more feared and respected than loved him. But in adolescence this pattern began to change as they spent more time together. They would take long drives in the country in which she chronicled the daily events of her life. He listened quietly, occasionally commenting on something she had said or criticizing her failures and admonishing her to do better. She looked up to him as the ideal male—powerful, responsible, and exacting. He liked things his way and would not tolerate deviance or rebellion. In these adolescent years, his opinion was a primary concern of hers. She always tried to please, dreading his reproach. His fault-finding nature scared her, yet she was equally determined to win him over.

In contrast to her older brother, who was always getting into trouble, Eileen was considered by everyone to be a "good girl." Her teachers liked her, and she did well in school. She dated the "right" boys, participated in the "proper" activities, and was the sort of child mothers would point out as exemplary. At times, this made her uncomfortable with her peers, but she also experienced the behavior as a source of pride.

In describing her childhood and adolescence, Eileen could not recall a single incident in which she had been in conflict with her parents or an authority figure. In fact, she was rarely involved in conflicts even with her friends. She was scared by her brother's freewheeling style and advised him to stop bringing embarrassment to his parents, "who had given him so much."

When the time came for Eileen to consider college (there was never any doubt she would go), she flirted with the idea of attending a large university in another state. On her parents' advice, she chose a local school. Wanting to be near her family, she persuaded herself that just as good an education could be had close to home as far away. She lived with her parents, and the next four years were a safe and comfortable extension of her high school experience.

In her senior year she began dating a young medical student who seemed like a perfect partner for her. He was practical, dependable, and high-minded, and he knew where he was going. His certainty attracted her immediately, and three months after she graduated, they married. Her parents naturally had approved of her choice, and the young couple moved into an apartment found by her mother.

In many ways, when I first met Tim he reminded me of my father—very serious and a little aloof. I wouldn't say we had a romance. Basically, we liked each other and were comfortable relating, but there was no courtship. It just seemed to happen. And when we decided to get married, it was the most practical decision. My parents really liked him, and I could see him fitting into the family. He and my father had a lot to talk about.

By Eileen's own admission, their marriage paralleled that of her parents. Tim was away long hours, and she found herself with little to do. Tim maintained his distance and

Eileen, who had seen this kind of arrangement all her life, never thought to question it. Tim played the "top dog" role, offering frequent criticism and admonishment. Eileen assumed the compliant position, anxious to please, but never quite measuring up. She began to feel more disappointed in herself as she failed to satisfy him. Despite her fears about looking for work, she saw the need to develop independent interests. She got a real ego-boost when she found a job teaching part time in a preschool. When the codirector spot at the adjoining daycare center was vacated, her self-doubts at first kept her from applying. Was she capable of managing an entire agency? The only way to find out was to try. Yet she feared a blow to her fledgling self-esteem. Uncharacteristically, she took the risk and was hired after the first interview.

The Loss of Inner Direction

In looking back at Eileen's personal history, we are struck by the important role her mother played in her life. As friend, confidante, advisor, and nurturer, she had had a hand in all Eileen's affairs. No private thoughts were encouraged, no boundaries tolerated. Every inner pang, every deep feeling was shared under the guise of love and concern. Even when Eileen felt the need to maintain her distance, she experienced guilt for not being completely open with her parents. Such a profound involvement creates either a symbiotic relationship that stifles individual development toward autonomy or an unhealthy overidentification with the mother that undermines the child's ability to make self-determined choices.

By intruding on every aspect of Eileen's life, her mother took from her the opportunity to both succeed and fail on her own. It is through this trial-and-error experience that children learn the satisfaction of mastery.

Eileen believed that if she expressed preferences that were different from her mother's, she would in fact be hurting her "best friend." Experience had taught her that when she said no or opposed her mother's direction, their relationship suffered. Love was withdrawn. Self-assertion was therefore associated with injuring her mother, a circumstance a good daughter would do anything to avoid. In effect, her behavior was ruled by the dictum, "Since she does everything for me, I cannot very well refuse her. And if I do, she will be hurt." It is clear that such an arrangement sacrifices the child's pressing need for self-direction in order to meet the requirements of someone else.

Approval Is the Number-One Priority

Eileen's mother was sweet and loving as long as her daughter acted in ways she thought best. The message Eileen understood was "Be a good girl or I won't love you." But beyond that withdrawal of love, Eileen was motivated by the additional pressure of guilt. When she was not "good" she was led to believe she had actually injured her mother in some important way. This produced feelings of wrongness which persuasively influenced her to bring her behavior into line. Losing love was bad enough; hurting Mom was intolerable.

Eileen's dependence on approval-seeking behavior was equaled only by her avoidance of disapproval. Her relationship with her father reflected this process. She would seek out his point of view and find herself expressing it to her friends as if it were her own. She dated boys in whom she was not particularly interested because they were acceptable to him. But in her compliant behavior she was also attempting to avoid his criticism—his sideways glance, furrowed brow, or chastising tone. These hurt her more than failure to win his approval through correct actions. What seemed like straightforward attempts to win acceptance were actually ploys to avoid disapproval.

Living Other People's Expectations

Eileen's life expectations were identical with her parents' because in fact they were borrowed from them. In learning to be the perfect daughter she had forgotten what *she* wanted for herself. She was living their script and acting in their play.

Eileen found that all her relationships reflected these early patterns. With her peers she was always anxious to please. Her schoolwork was a constant attempt to meet the expectations of her teachers. In new situations she would think to herself, "How does this person want me to be?" She tailored her behavior to fit what she believed was the expectation. These responses were not processed consciously. In fact, the only time she was aware of this pattern was when she failed to win someone's approval or affection.

In her marriage she tried to please her husband, win his love and approval, and avoid his censure. If he wanted a dutiful wife—a supportive, passive, domestic type—then that's what she would be. If he preferred an intellectual peer or a charming companion to wear on his arm, she would work hard to be those things. Occasionally she resented this endless pressure and her husband as well, but these singular moments were usually followed by periods of self-reproach for failing to be what he wanted.

Work was no different. Her behavior was shaped by the expectations of her boss, the board of directors, and even her staff. Her constant endeavor to please everyone was only partially successful. And the effort was exhausting.

Because she was afraid of disappointing, she found it difficult to use the authority inherent in her administrative position. She could not say "no" or draw the line when necessary. Her "good girl" training did not prepare her for assertive behavior, and she was afraid of appearing harsh or arbitrary. As long as she had no power, her compliant tendencies were only a nuisance. Put in a position of authority, she felt paralyzed.

Disappointment in Self

To the question "What do *you* want?" Eileen had very little to say. After thirty-one years, she was still trying to please, still trying to measure up to the expectations of others. In truth she did not know what she wanted because her focus had always been away from herself. This external orientation left her a stranger to her own needs and preferences, and, in a broader sense, to her own nature. Without someone else to react to she was lost. In brief periods of introspection she always felt empty and disappointed in herself. Her solution was to try harder to be the good daughter, the perfect boss, the ideal wife. But these efforts were counterproductive. They never changed her deep-seated feelings.

Eileen was disappointed in herself for failing to meet the demands of those around her. But their expectations were not of her making and so inevitably she had to falter. She was attempting to live her life like a painter who merely colors in the outlines drawn by someone else. There is no inspiration in such an exercise. It is prosaic and spiritless. No wonder she experienced disappointment.

When Eileen felt resentment toward others for their demands, real or imagined, she censored those feelings and turned them back on herself. So afraid was she of her own accumulated anger that she converted it to disappointment in self as a means of avoiding its expression. Thus, instead of venting anger at her mother for expecting a daily telephone call, Eileen condemned herself. "If I were a loyal daughter," she thought, "I wouldn't resent calling her."

To some extent, her self-disappointment was also a reflection of her parents' response when she had failed to satisfy them as a child. In effect, she had "internalized" their reaction and was now playing their former roles in her own drama. She was both "disappointing" and "disappointed." Convoluted as this turnaround may seem at first glance, it is quite common. The admonishing voice of our parents remains within us long after we separate from them. It becomes our own reproving inner surrogate, advising us that we should have known better, tried harder, and so forth. In the language of transactional analysis, this voice is the "critical parent"; in psychoanalysis, the superego; in religion, the conscience. Whatever we call the judgmental arbiter, it carries the stamp of our parents' particular fault-finding style. If they expressed anger at our failings, we will likely use the same tactic on ourselves. If they showed letdown...well, the result is obvious. For Eileen, dissatisfaction in self was the flip side of her parents' disappointment in her.

The Acquiescent Style in Retrospect

The acquiescent style is based on one desire: to meet the expectations of other people. When put this simply, such behavior sounds foolish and absurd. But due to the circumstances of their personal histories, compliant individuals come to believe that the approval of others is a necessary ingredient in their interpersonal lives. Without approval they doubt themselves and feel directionless. Yet seeking validation exclusively from others undermines their integrity and sense of self. They lose both ways.

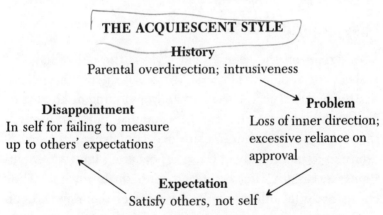

THE ACQUIESCENT STYLE

History
Parental overdirection; intrusiveness

Disappointment
In self for failing to measure
up to others' expectations

Problem
Loss of inner direction;
excessive reliance on
approval

Expectation
Satisfy others, not self

This style inevitably results in disappointment because one cannot please all the people all the time. It is difficult enough to meet one's own expectations. Compliant individuals, trying to accomplish the impossible, end up pleasing no one, especially not themselves. It is a self-defeating and self-perpetuating pattern of behavior which ends in despair.

As with all disappointment, prevention requires reevaluation of the basic expectation and the lifewish underlying it. The profound desire to be loved unconditionally characterizes all acquiescent personalities. Because approval was historically linked to "correct" behavior, they long for acceptance and affection with no strings attached. Feeling unworthy of such love, they are trapped. Since they believe they can only win the validating affection of others through pleasing and compliant behavior, they can never find the unqualified acceptance they crave. Giving up the lifewish to be loved unconditionally and risking disapproval by taking independent action according to internal needs provides the exit from this impasse.

Disappointing Others

A variant on the acquiescent style is the individual who is always disappointing others. Much like Eileen, this person has been raised in an overdirected environment characterized by high expectation and parental manipulation through the display and withdrawal of love. But where Eileen attempted to meet many of these expectations (and was sometimes successful), disappointing individuals do not. They consistently let other people down, rarely coming through at the critical moment and frustrating all who depend on them. It is as if their behavior is saying, "You see, I told you not to expect anything from me. I can't give you what you need!"

Examples: The spouse who retreats into himself in response to his wife's impending operation; the daughter who fails to show up for her parents' twenty-fifth wedding anniversary after promising to help with the food preparation; the worker who makes a commitment to do a special job and reneges on the agreement belatedly.

These disappointing individuals are of two types: those who make promises and fail to keep them, and those who simply withdraw from recognized expectation without offering false pretense. But this difference is one of form, not substance. Both have given up on their ability to meet the expectations of significant others. Too self-absorbed, burdened, or thwarted, they have historically been unable to satisfy the expectations of their parents, and this view of themselves as "disappointing children" has stayed with them. It is a "loser" identity, distinguished by a deeply rooted sense of personal inadequacy. Rather than risk failing in their efforts, they choose not to make the attempt in the first place, hence insuring a continuing style of failure followed by feelings of deficiency.

Most of these disappointing individuals find such comfort in their familiar ne'er-do-well role that they have little impetus for change. By throwing off the cloak of others' expectations through their repeated failure to come through, they have chiseled out a safe niche for themselves. No one realistically expects anything from them, and they have fulfilled their childhood "script" to perfection. Yet despite the security of their position, they are always unhappy and plagued by self-doubt. In effect, they are afraid of succeeding as well as failing, since success brings with it the expectation of continued accomplishment.

CHAPTER **8**

The Deprived Style

> *A child forsaken, waking suddenly,*
> *Whose gaze afeard on all things round doth rove,*
> *And seeth only that it cannot see*
> *The meeting eyes of love.*
>
> George Eliot

Expect the worst! Catastrophe, loss, disease, humiliation—
anticipate them all. Think of the blessed relief you'll experience should the outcome be more favorable. And if it is
not, at least you'll be prepared for any contingency. This is
the strategy of the person who has been severely wounded
by disappointment in childhood. He or she walks through
the world hoping to avoid a repetition of history by anticipating the negative event. The chosen remedy is unfortunate
because it distorts perception. Expecting a piano to fall on
your head tends to put quite a crook in the neck. You can't
see straight anymore. Always looking skyward, you lose perspective, swept up by fears and wariness. Comedian George
Burns humorously describes such a person as "a man who
feels bad when he feels good for fear he'll feel worse when
he feels better."

You probably know people like this. Pessimism is the only

perspective that feels comfortable to them because their thinking is based on two incorrigible premises: "Life is pain" and "You never get what you want." Although their world view is ostensibly focused on preventing disappointment, they are profoundly disillusioned. Their cynical nihilism is a defense against ever being hurt or let down. So deep and early is the original disappointment that the individual's perspective is terribly tainted by childhood history. To risk disappointment is to possibly reconnect with the primary pain of the past, a possibility feared above all others. I have called this pattern of disappointment the deprived style because it reflects the individual's most basic feeling about life.

Peter's Story

Peter, a heavy-drinking, forty-five-year-old architect, is the sort of man you try to avoid even in an elevator. Although he has a clever, acerbic wit, a bitterness so palpable it nearly feels contagious underlies his satirical facade and keeps people at bay.

After twelve years of marriage, his wife announced her desire for a divorce. At first he protested, but when she began dating other men, he quietly accepted her request. After their separation, he drew into himself, took to drinking in the afternoons to ease his loneliness, and relinquished all pleasurable activity. He became despairing and world weary, describing himself as "jaded." He gave the impression of an old man just waiting out his last few years. With the death of his ambition and no clear life goals, he was merely concerned with getting through the day. He and his wife had no children. He rarely saw his family, who lived two thousand miles away. He was a man alone, who seemed—at least for the moment—to want to keep it that way.

To the observing eye, Peter appeared frail, as if his level of energy was insufficient to meet the stress of living. His legs in particular were spindly and weak, offering his torso only marginal support. His feet were bony and narrow, creating the same impression. The white skin of his face was sallow and without tone. His body was elongated and thin, and his musculature seemed underdeveloped in general. When he stood up, his shoulders stooped and his chest collapsed into itself. His body seemed to say it had difficulty standing firmly on its own two feet. There was a deprived quality to it, as if he had not received enough life energy.

Further observation revealed that Peter hardly exerted himself when breathing. His respiration had the particular characteristics associated with disappointment. He took in air in a tentative manner without assertion, and his torso showed minimal movement, particularly in the exhalation phase. His eyes held a longing, soulful expression with a slight trace of acrimony. There was a stubborn quality to his set jaw. He looked determined and defiant, a man who willed himself through difficult times to compensate for a body that could not handle stress. There was nothing soft about his physique. It seemed rock-hard, as if shaped by loneliness and deprivation.

Peter's feelings about himself supported these impressions. He believed no one could be trusted: "Sooner or later they turn on you or abandon you for greener pastures." He was bitter about his wife's treatment of him, but his attitude was resigned: "What can you expect? Relationships are just

arrangements in which people use each other until they
become bored and split. It's inevitable." From Peter's point
of view it made no sense to show vulnerability to your partner. She would simply use it against you at another time:
"We don't really need anyone else but ourselves. We carry
around this myth that we must be surrounded by other
people when, in reality, we can get along perfectly well
alone." And, of course, Peter's life of isolation was penetrated
by few friends and no real intimates. He had modest material
and interpersonal needs, and managed when others couldn't
because he required so little. And he expected even less
from life. He anticipated the worst and usually got it. His
vision of the world as a bleak landscape devoid of sweetness
was self-fulfilling. He had it all figured out. But he was
miserable and drinking himself into oblivion.

At first glance Peter's difficulties seem merely a poor adjustment to his wrecked marriage. But his history reveals
that he was not simply reacting to the pain of current bruises.
He had struggled his whole life with the enduring pain of
isolation and disappointment. His present situation was a
mirror of his past.

A Loveless Childhood

The fourth and last child of immigrant parents, Peter was
born at an inopportune time. Shortly after his birth, his
father's small store went bankrupt, and his mother was forced
to find employment to supplement the family income. Peter's oldest sister took care of him indifferently, leaving him
alone for long periods. His older brother bullied him while

his parents ignored his urgent protests. He had the impression, in fact, that they thought he complained too much, and after a while he gave up seeking their intervention. He felt isolated within the family. He was not close to any of his other siblings, and he often feared that no one wanted to spend time with him. He felt especially neglected by his mother, who was always too busy to look after his needs. Once she had failed to come to a play in which he had a principal role. He was heartbroken, but did not even mention the event when he came home.

To deal with his sense of deprivation and loss, Peter created a fantasy world over which he ruled as king. He gave himself in fantasy what he was unable to get in reality. Because he had received such minimal affection and care, he found himself looking everywhere for signs of reassurance. He described himself as a clinging and dependent child. He followed his sisters around but was usually ostracized by them. His brother simply used him as a target for his own frustrations.

Peter's memory of the past was startlingly clear and fresh. He remembered dozens of incidents in which he had felt emotionally hurt. Was he maintaining some sort of scorecard even now? He recalled the hand-me-down clothes from his brother and cousins, which were always too big and made him feel strangely insignificant. He thought of the numerous promises made by his parents and never fulfilled. He remembered these things not with hurt and longing but without emotion, as if they were the events of someone else's life. There was a stoic detachment that was odd and out of place.

By age seven Peter had ceased his clinging behavior and

had withdrawn into himself. He no longer followed his sisters or bothered his brother. He rarely asked for anything. He began to take a certain pride in needing less than his siblings. He felt righteous in his independence. His parents implied that they considered his new behavior constructive and a sign of maturity. At school he maintained his isolation. He felt different from his peers. Although he acted calm and in control, he really felt overwhelmed by social pressures. Yet he confided in no one.

Adolescence brought only minor changes in this pattern. He remained isolated and began to develop skills in the fine arts. He spent long hours sketching pictures of men in boxes and figures reaching out into space. These wonderfully detailed drawings expressed his deepest feelings. The boxes represented the sense of enclosed isolation that separated him from others. Reaching out reflected his deep need to make contact despite the barriers he experienced around him.

Relationships with the opposite sex were also difficult. Peter seemed to find himself struggling continually to maintain unrequited love affairs. He sought out young women who were not interested in him and pined away writing poems and sketching their faces. Peter rejected those who paid him any attention. If they were interested in him, how desirable could they be? Following the classic Groucho Marx line, "I wouldn't join any club that would have me as a member," he discounted potential partners on the basis of their poor taste. He was undesirable. They must be too.

Peter chose to pursue a career as an architect. In his early adulthood, he worked very hard to perfect his craft. This was done at the expense of a personal life. He continued to remain aloof, although he had many business acquaintances whom he counted among his friends. In his early thirties he met Lisa, who worked in the office of one of his associates. He struck up a friendship immediately, but it was she who pursued him. After two years they decided to marry. It was the sort of relationship that friends considered ideal. They shared the same profession, a devotion to their work, and similar lifestyles. Their temperaments were also alike—low-keyed and mild. Not as apparent to onlookers was the paucity of affection they gave each other. Self-disclosure was rare, and sharing feelings of vulnerability inconceivable. They were emotionally distant "intimate" partners. Over the years the distance between them grew. Finally, aware of the irreparable gap between them, Lisa made a last attempt to reach out to him. She asked that they see a therapist together. Peter acknowledged their problem but refused counseling, unwilling to change the way he related to her. For him intimate contact was painful, risky, and unfamiliar. Eventually they separated. She found another partner. He withdrew further into himself.

The Broken Heart

Infancy is a time of great vulnerability. Lying on its back, unable to turn its tiny body or even raise its head to look at the new world, the newborn is a study in helplessness. It relies entirely on the care and nurturance of its parents. If there is some profound disturbance or pattern of abuse in the contact or nursing of the infant, its sense of well-being is compromised. The effect of that disruption—if it is intense—will ripple like a chain reaction through all the developmental stages of the child and into adulthood.

For the young child, bodily connection to the mother is a manifestation of maternal love. To be held is to be protected and nurtured. Although we lack all the details of his early history, there is reason to believe that Peter suffered some sort of interruption in the early nurturing phase. When his mother went to work, his care was entrusted to his oldest sister, who found the task burdensome. He was prematurely expected to look after himself. His sense of deprivation left him empty and disconsolate. Did anyone really care? If he left home, would his family even bother to search for him? Would anyone miss him? In truth, Peter suffered from a broken heart.

Building Walls as a Lifestyle

Peter made peace with his deprivation by denying his needs. This was strategy for survival. He had been bitterly disappointed time and again. In order to diminish his pain and prevent its recurrence, he removed himself from the cause of his troubles: his own needs. If he required nothing, he could not be disappointed. It was a simple solution for which he paid dearly, but it was the most effective and, perhaps, the only viable remedy open to him.

What began as a psychological defense against disappointment and loss became a lifestyle. Eventually Peter began to lose access to his deeper feelings. To avoid further pain he closed off his heart. He thought of love as cheap sentiment or a euphemism for sex. He was able to relate only on the most superficial level. Intimacy was out of the question. This is why his marriage ultimately failed. He would not allow another person in, afraid his neediness would be overwhelming. If he were rejected, the old feelings of deprivation and loss might be reawakened. He preferred a relationship without risk, a passionless and utilitarian arrangement that would be convenient for both parties.

Peter's life was filled with the idiosyncrasies of self-denial. Whereas in the past his parents had been the agents of his deprivation, now, ironically, he chose to deny himself. The deprived identity became an ingrained behavioral pattern. He drove an old car that was always breaking down, even though he could afford something more reliable. He lived in a crowded studio apartment which barely permitted him space for a drafting table. He rarely bought himself anything of value and continued to wear old, shabby clothing except at work. Money was not the issue. Peter just felt uncomfortable providing for himself. Anything beyond bare-bones necessity he considered indulgent.

The pattern carried over into other areas. He never allowed himself pleasurable experiences. He took vacations infrequently. It would never occur to him to plan a weekend at a resort or spend a night on the town. He avoided situations that might give him recognition or praise. These experiences made him feel uncomfortable and awkward. He did not know how to respond to compliments or acknowledgment. On one occasion, he left a community meeting early because he suspected a friend was going to praise him publicly for work he had done. It was not humility that drove him away, but rather anxiety with any form of acclamation.

All of Peter's actions were designed to avoid the possibility of further disappointment, the hallmark of the deprived style. Below is a graphic representation of his experience:

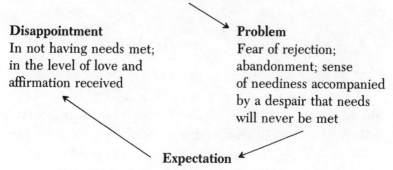

THE DEPRIVED STYLE

History
Emotional and physical deprivation

Disappointment
In not having needs met;
in the level of love and
affirmation received

Problem
Fear of rejection;
abandonment; sense
of neediness accompanied
by a despair that needs
will never be met

Expectation
Expect the worst (defense against feeling hurt)

Underlying the negative expectation is the lifewish never to be hurt again. But beyond this defensive wish looms a greater and more urgent desire: to get all one's emotional needs met without having to risk asking for help. Gratification of this unconscious fantasy represents an "undoing" of the deprivation experience by providing the individual with unsolicited nurturance, solid proof that he or she is deserving of the love so long denied. Deprived persons do not dare allow this thought into consciousness because recognition calls up the pain of having been unloved. The defensive wish and expectation is, therefore, substituted as a safer alternative, an attempt to avoid any further disappointment.

To move out of this self-perpetuating pattern, these individuals must acknowledge their profound needs for love and risk asserting them. They must reach out to others despite deep fears of rejection, and in this way learn that they can survive the ravages of disappointment. Only by taking this chance can they find the caring and affection that has eluded them for so long.

Another Deprived Style: The Romantic

Emotional deprivation in the attachment between parent and child does not always create an individual who expects the worst. Another defense can be used. In response to the deprived condition, the child may indulge in extensive fantasy, reordering the universe in a more tolerable manner. As the individual grows, he or she maintains these fantasies in the culturally acceptable form of romantic or idealistic beliefs. Naturally, not everyone with romantic notions fits into this group. Impassioned thoughts may be the product of uncommon personal traits, for example, a highly developed imagination or a marked sensitivity to the environment. There are those, however, whose very character is built on a longing for life to fulfill idealized myths, the dreamy-eyed souls who hold fast to their storybook perspective in the face of obvious contradicting facts. Such individuals are constantly let down when events fall short of their sentimental anticipations. They show a pattern of disappointment I call the romantic style.

Examples of romantic notions: "And it all ended happily ever after"; "Someone will come along and save me from the mess I've made of my life"; "Love is all one needs"; "I don't have to compromise"; "My mother really loved me in her own way."

The romantic style is characterized by a histrionic view of the world in which all aspects of relationship are colored by passion and ardor. These individuals are in love with love. They crave experiences in which the heart palpitates with feverish desire or longing and they indulge in ill-fated love affairs which leave them in paroxysms of regret. They expect their partners to share their flammable feelings and are prone to cling to their anguish long after a relationship has ended. To people who never got enough love, that four-letter word is magical. Their lives are quests to gain this treasure, but feeling fundamentally undeserving and fearful of attachment, they sabotage intimacy. Their lifewish is for true love to save them—the obvious antidote to the unbearable deprivation of early life. When it does not happen, they seem to relish their tragic condition.

The life expectations of the romantic lean heavily on the themes of cruel fate, the loneliness and purity of isolation, and, above all, the redemption of love. Filled with hyperbole and melodrama, these unrealistic anticipations are futile. Romantic individuals are, therefore, continually disappointed. But a tragic world view is so vital to their sense of identity that they are usually unwilling to adapt to a more grounded approach to life. It is as if they are enamored of the deprivation and yearning pattern begun in their first few years. Its anguished overtones sustain them and they are drawn to the martyr role that accompanies their suffering. They clearly prefer disappointment to the loss of their passion.

The romantic perspective, entrenched as it is in the dual

sensibilities of love and tragedy, makes for good reading. Indeed, literature overflows with tales of unrequited love, twists of fate, and forsaken hearts. For that matter, so do the soap operas and dime-store magazines. But the style is ill-suited for living because it produces excessive expectations. Eventually these extravagant anticipations create enough chronic disappointment to threaten the romantic soul which thrives on adversity. When this happens, even visions of Canaan cannot prevent the ensuing depression and despair.

CHAPTER 9

The Self-Important Style

Self-love is the greatest of all flatterers.

François,
Duc de La Rochefoucauld

Jan and Jonathan are successful by most American standards. They are both professionals with graduate degrees, employed in good jobs, materially comfortable, enviably attractive and intelligent, and in good health. Yet, despite their good fortune, one is left with the impression that they are deeply disappointed in their lives.

Jonathan:

> I know I'm better off than the average worker whose job may be cut tomorrow, but somehow that doesn't make me feel better. Jan and I have been working our butts off for a half-dozen years now and we are still struggling to get what we always assumed we'd have. Even with two incomes, we can't afford a house in the city. I'm working as hard as my father did without nearly as much to show for it.

Jan:

I grew up in an affluent suburb where all my friends went to camp, every family had two cars and a maid, and all the kids had access to their mothers' credit cards. I expected at least the same for myself. True, I have a nice apartment, but it's really too small. I'd like to buy a second place in the country but can only afford the land without the house. I'm not even sure I want a child because the cost of good daycare and private school education is so prohibitive.

Don't get me wrong. Jonathan and I are not poor. We can manage without scrimping. But we both work hard and don't have much to show for it. It doesn't seem fair. With taxes and daily expenses, we can't afford the important extras that we should be entitled to.

Disappointment in the level of material acquisition is only part of their story. Jan complains of "anonymity" in her huge law firm, "retarded advancement," and lack of genuine recognition for "the blood-and-guts sacrifices I've made." Jonathan resents "being lost" in the large bureaucracy and the lack of acknowledgment by his superiors.

Jonathan:

I'll be blunt. I don't like being just a number in a large agency. I want people to see how special I am and not shrug me off as another Tom, Dick, or Harry. The worst thing about working in the public sphere is that individuals are taken for granted. They're interchangeable parts.

When I first began working in Public Health, fresh out of graduate school with some pretty decent ideas, I thought I would set the place on fire. But as it turned out no one in a position of power wanted to use them or even try them out on a small scale. Since then I've learned not to waste my energy, but it still galls me.

Jan:

I seem to be moving up through the ranks at work at about the same speed as everyone else. That's what bothers me. I don't like the position of being "another bright, up-and-coming lawyer." I want them to acknowledge that my energies and talents are unique and to know I'm someone special.

Jan's and Jonathan's complaints seem legitimate enough. In a period of diminishing economic opportunity and greater competition (brought on in part by the coming of age of the huge postwar baby cohort), disappointments in the level of material wealth and the rate of career advancement are commonplace. But if we look a little deeper, we find that their story is more complex. Both Jan and Jonathan fit into a third type of disappointment pattern, the self-important style. These individuals view themselves as special and therefore different from others. They expect the world to recognize their superiority and to treat them accordingly. When it invariably does not, they are surprised and let down. Having grown up in families that accorded them favored status, they believe the world owes them something. They dislike being mere faces in the crowd. They are obsessed with "making it," and their worst fear is that they will live undistinguished lives of no import. They crave attention and work hard to succeed but are rarely satisfied with their triumphs.

One-Sided Relationships

Nowhere is the self-important style so problematic as in relationships which require mutuality and shared affection to survive. Self-important individuals have great difficulty establishing a reciprocal arrangement with their partners.

They are used to being on top, exercising prerogatives, and receiving favored treatment. They are prone to establish one-sided "instrumental" relationships, viewing their lovers as the source of their narcissistic supplies. Their self-absorption prevents recognition of their partners' needs and precludes giving back in equal measure.

When two self-important types are drawn to each other, it is not long before an emotional gulf develops between them. Although each expects the other to assume the provider role, neither is willing to take it on.

After five years of marriage, Jan and Jonathan found themselves in this bleak situation. Originally attracted to each other by their similar natures, they soon learned that their alikeness also created problems. Both were demanding, egocentric, and competitive. Both made their careers top priority and were afraid of the other holding them back. When they were in open conflict—which was often—neither was able to see their partner's position. Each felt the other was selfish and uncaring.

Jan:

> The first few years of our marriage were a constant battle. We were at each other's throats. I think we were both disappointed in how little we got from each other. I know I was. I always expected my husband would give me respect and attention. Jonathan just didn't come through. He's too involved with his career and his image. He doesn't seem really interested in me. He resents my having needs, especially if they interfere with his plans. He wants me to take care of him, but he won't do the same for me.

Jonathan:

> My biggest gripe with Jan is that she's too demanding. She's always asking for attention in one way or another. And when

she doesn't get it, there's hell to pay. One time she was upset by a situation at work and I was preoccupied with something else. She made such a big stink about it you'd think I had done something dreadful. I can't tell you the number of times she's ignored me when I needed her.

Like many couples, Jan and Jonathan were quick to notice the other's problems and blind to the same processes in themselves. Each felt entitled to special treatment, yet neither was willing to provide it. Accustomed to being on the receiving end all their lives, the "giving" role was unfamiliar and artificial.

Extramarital Affairs: Convenient Narcissistic Supplies

Several years into their marriage, Jan began to feel depressed and developed intestinal problems. Inside herself she experienced an intense feeling of hurt and disregard. She felt invalidated by her husband and turned to other relationships with friends and colleagues at work. But no one was able to supply the degree and intensity of attention she craved. She resolved the situation by having an affair with one of the young lawyers in her office. Although she considered him less than an equal in status and attractiveness, he was just what she needed: a man who would clearly see her uniqueness and appreciate her precisely because of it.

An extramarital tryst is nothing if not a source of narcissistic supplies. Its temporal, electric qualities are a bromide for feelings of low self-esteem and unattractiveness. So it was for Jan. She found herself more and more drawn to her lover, and her marriage, already badly strained, was stretched to new boundaries of aloofness. She spent longer periods away from Jonathan, ostensibly at her office.

Gradually her husband began to recognize something had changed. He suspected her of other involvements but had no information to support his intuition. Finally one evening he overheard her on the phone with her lover. He was shocked. Despite their drifting from each other, he had never expected her to look for someone else. He felt hurt and in some curious way envious, but he hid both these emotions behind a facade of muted resentment. He became sarcastic and ironic, pretending to be above the bitter hostility that brooded within him. In response, Jan was contrite. She felt guilty but not wrong for seeking a companion who would gratify her needs. Yet the pressure of maintaining two re-lationships and the ever-growing realization that her lover was only a vehicle for her sexual desire. Several months later, she ended the liaison.

But Jonathan held onto his resentment. He would not forgive her. He experienced Jan's actions as an injury to him, a way to drag him through the mud and intentionally demean him. He could not see her behavior as a function of her own needs. Like a child, he perceived every event only in terms of its influence on him.

Months later, after time had cooled the intensity of his feelings and the two of them were again relating in their usual manner, he took up with another woman. The affair lasted only a few weeks and Jan never found out about it. Jonathan's motivation was complex. He acted partially out of revenge, but his primitive desire for retribution did not fully explain the whirlwind of emotions he felt in the pit of his stomach. Her affair had knocked him off his pedestal and reduced him to a cuckold. Haunted by the thought that he was just another sap, he sought a way to neutralize these feelings. The interest of another woman inflated his injured sense of self and gave him back his personal respect.

Early History: A Special Role

Jan was the oldest of two daughters in a well-to-do family. She grew up in a sheltered suburban community and attended local schools until she went off to a selective eastern women's college. As the first grandchild in her family, her birth was met with great anticipation. She was seen as an exceptional child, fussed over and indulged with every affection. Her mother was delighted with the commotion her daughter caused. She saw Jan's specialness as an appropriate reflection of herself.

The first four years of Jan's life continued in this vein. No matter how commonplace her achievements, whatever she did was noted and praised. She was dressed up in pretty clothes, taught sophisticated stories and songs, and presented with countless gifts and toys so that her room resembled an F.A.O. Schwarz display before Christmas.

When she was four, the pattern changed. Her sister was born and her mother's attentions were directed elsewhere. The loss might have been traumatic had not another event occurred simultaneously. Her father was in a serious automobile accident, and his recovery required a long convalescence at home. This event provided Jan with an even better companion than her mother. Her father had little to do but observe his daughter, who delighted him with her precocious wit and charm. Jan became "Daddy's little girl"— his obvious favorite.

But as her father recovered and returned to work, she lost her captive and appreciative audience. Although she understood that he was compelled to earn a living, she felt hurt and abandoned by his abrupt departure, and deeply disappointed that her special relationship had been dissolved. Nevertheless, she maintained her favored role in the family. Admired and imitated by her younger sister and cousins, she did well in school and was doted on by her piano and ballet teachers. But the situation was not as ideal as it seemed. Although her parents did not interfere with her emerging sense of independence and gratified her material needs, their primary concern was how she reflected on them. Their attentiveness and praise were motivated not only by their love but by a personal investment in her actions and achievements. They saw her as a representation of themselves and their family, not as an individual unto herself.

As Jan matured, she recognized that the specialness she now craved and regarded as her right was highly conditional. When she did not perform well, her parents seemed less interested in her. Not that they chastised or admonished. They rewarded her achievements and dismissed her failures as aberrations. But as reasonable as their behavior seemed to them, it caused problems for her.

The truth of her situation was that her feelings of doubt, anxiety, and inadequacy—potential obstacles to her performance—were unacceptable and probably uncomfortable to her parents. They tried to extinguish them by acting as if they did not exist. But Jan needed to express her doubts and get assurance that she was okay despite her imperfections. In fact, her mother's failure to accept her feelings of vulnerability left her wondering whether her parents would continue to love her if she were unsuccessful and reflected poorly on them.

To resolve her disappointment in their response and to meet their expectations for high performance, she learned to hold her anxieties in check through determination and stubborn self-control. She gave up trying to get acknowledgment of her feelings of inadequacy and became critical of them. She would not tolerate their expression. She became rigid and unyielding, her softer emotions buried and inaccessible. Her range of feeling was sacrificed for the sake of control. She rarely felt anxious but neither did she experience joy or lofty emotion.

As she approached adulthood, armored against her own doubts and apprehensions, she found it harder to relax, slow down, and be receptive to the world around her. Her ability to maintain friendships suffered. She had difficulty feeling empathy and tenderness for those close to her. Her exaggerated sense of self-importance—cultivated by her family—reasserted itself along with the corollary belief that she deserved her special status. She saw herself as unique and superior and her vanity required a diet of constant attention and favored treatment.

Jonathan's background was not so different from Jan's. He was the only son and oldest child in a middle-class family. Like Jan he received a great deal of early attention and was clearly his parents' favorite. He was shown off to relatives and neighbors and treated like a prize. He had an especially close relationship with his mother of which even his father

seemed covetous. There was an adult flavor to their interaction. He was her "little man," and a mild sexual flirtation
could be detected between them.

His parents maintained high expectations for him. They
applauded his achievements at school, and were particularly
proud of the fact that he assumed a leadership role among
his peers. He was class president, editor of the school newspaper, captain of the team. On the occasions when he failed
to do well, he felt painfully humiliated. For Jonathan any
flaw in performance was experienced as failure. He knew
that his mother in particular would be disappointed. Unlike
Jan's parents, she did not hesitate in criticizing his failures.
He wanted to avoid these unpleasant confrontations as well
as maintain the pleasure of reporting his triumphs. Intuitively he recognized that she was enormously invested in
his success. Her undisguised scorn of those who were unsuccessful and her admiration of individuals who had distinguished themselves were relative constants in her
conversations with him. He knew his mother felt a gain in
stature as a result of his achievements. In fact, sometimes
he thought that her expectations for him were designed to
meet her wishes exclusively.

> I enjoy it when my mother gets off on my successes. It's amusing
> to me that she's so involved in what I do. Occasionally, though,
> she acts like the classic stage mother. She "pushes" me for her
> benefit. She'd never admit it, but she's relating to my success
> as if it were hers. She's not recognizing me in a real way, but
> only as a reflection of her. Then I feel used!

Every child must contend with the dilemmas posed by
parental expectations. For Jonathan, the pressures to be a
"success" were much greater than, for example, the expectations that he be "moral," "artistic," or "sweet." The result

was that by adolescence he had locked himself into a particular path and by early adulthood his own expectations for success exceeded even his mother's. This choice required determination and self-control. At college and graduate school, he studied hard and allowed few diversions. Most of his energy was devoted to work; his marriage and friendships played a comparatively minor role except as they supported his strivings.

He became increasingly absorbed in himself. He spent a great deal of time and effort on his personal appearance. His clothing, his hair style, and physical condition were important to him, and he was keenly aware of the image he projected although he took pains to appear casual about it. His bearing suggested pride and superiority, but there was also a hint of restraint in it. He appeared bound by his own needs for control and performance.

Jan and Jonathan were two of a kind. Though the details of their history differed, the patterns were remarkably similar. Both maintained a privileged position in their respective families, which directly influenced their inflated sense of self-importance. Each was the recipient of abundant material gratification, evoking feelings of entitlement. Both experienced high expectations for achievement and a loss of parental approval when they failed, a situation which led them to equate performance with personal worth. And each had a strong relationship with the opposite-sex parent that fed their motivation to meet parental expectations.

Misguided Astronomers

Self-important individuals are engrossed in themselves. They like nothing more than to talk about the details of their lives, regardless of how mundane, and they seem to think that others are equally interested. They are poor listeners who often redirect the subject of discussion back to their own exploits. They are frequently exhibitionistic in an attempt to gain attention and praise.

Some are drawn to intensive psychotherapy by the constant failure of their relationships, but many come simply to gain the fixed regard of another human being. What could be more satisfying than sitting with an individual whose sole function is to listen and sort through the principal experiences of one's life? That much scrutiny is a covert affirmation of specialness. No wonder self-important individuals are found in large numbers among the "experience junkies" who try every new psychological technique in the name of personal growth. Most are there not to change for the better but to feed their egocentricity. They crave the focus on self for its own sake.

Like misguided astronomers, self-important types believe the universe revolves around their personal planet. To shift their frame of reference from "me" to "you" requires maximum effort. In couple therapy, for example, they usually have problems with the "role reversal" exercise in which each partner takes the other's viewpoint. They are too self-engrossed to recognize alternative ways of thinking, and they are quick to classify as foes those who do not support their position.

Disappointment and the Self-Important Style

The self-important style leads ineluctably to chronic disappointment because it is based on exaggerated assumptions about one's self which society is expected to mirror. An inflated sense of personal worth produces expectations that are grandiose. Self-important individuals often believe they can succeed where others have failed, that nothing can stop them, and that they will always get what they want. But there is one expectation larger than all the rest—the belief that they are *entitled* to unusual privilege without assuming reciprocal responsibilities. This idea crudely translates to "I expect to get what I want because *I* want it!" Such an inflated attitude is a far cry from the humble thoughts of the "deprived" individual. Self-important types represent the other extreme. They are convinced their specialness justifies a positive response to their request for a bank loan, college application, or marriage proposal. Inevitably, they are let down when their overblown wishes are shattered by reality or when society fails to recognize their claims.

Relationships, however, are where the greatest disappointments occur. These individuals see relationships as an arena in which to gain admiration and attention. They exploit intimacy for their own ends, but ultimately they are disappointed. Usually one of two scenarios occurs:

1. The partner, feeling used, refuses to provide any more approbation, and often abruptly ends the relationship.
2. The self-important individual disparages both the partner and quality of attention received. He or she withdraws, hoping to find another who will provide satisfaction. After countless frustrations, the disappointment reaches chronic proportions and the individual retreats further into self.

To love another being requires surrendering to feeling and transcending one's own boundaries. It means yielding to a larger purpose, a union greater than the self. And it demands giving for its own pleasure without concern for what is to be gained. Consumed by their needs for achievement, self-control, and constant attention, these people do poorly at love. And because love is received in proportion to one's capacity to give it, in the end their greatest disappointment is their inability to open their hearts.

THE SELF-IMPORTANT STYLE

History
Favored family position;
high level of gratification;
high level of expectation

Disappointment
In loss of specialness; in not getting what one rightfully deserves

Problem
Grandiose sense of self; self-worth linked to performance

Expectation
To be entitled to special treatment; to get continual gratification

The self-important style, characterized by grandiose expectations, is based on the lifewish to be special. To surrender that illusory desire, these individuals must accept their ordinariness and develop a more balanced picture of themselves. It is not an easy solution. For them, ordinary means worthless. I remember the words of one of my patients who remarked despairingly, "To see myself as an average person like everyone else is to give up my identity." But recognizing the characteristics of all humanity in oneself enlarges rather than shrinks identity. Everyone of us is a combination of common and special qualities. We are capable of both greatness and triviality. Those who place themselves above all others are seeing only half the picture.

Before indulging in aggrandizement, the self-important individual would do well to take a closer look at the limitations of the human condition. For all our diverseness and productivity, we have yet to answer the most fundamental questions: "Why do we live?" and "What follows life?" And despite the combined knowledge of generations, we have not found a means to eradicate violence and war. We are a highly fallible, suggestible and corruptible species, insignificant in the larger scheme of the universe. When we consider that our sun is only one star among a hundred billion others in this galaxy alone, and that there are numberless other galaxies, the shallowness of our daily concerns is inescapable. This perspective dwarfs the grandiosity of self-important individuals and renders it absurd.

CHAPTER 10

Expectation: The Key to Preventing Disappointment

Nothing is as good as it seems beforehand.
George Eliot

The quality of our expectations determines the quality of our actions.
André Grodin

Expectation is a puzzling phenomenon. It has the capacity to both enlarge and diminish our experience. It can inspire us to superhuman feats beyond the realm of scientific knowledge, or it can severely limit our lives to the commonplace. It can heal the sick and give heart to the hopeless, but it may just as easily distract our perceptions and dull our awareness.

The influence of expectation is seen in daily events. One patient is given medication for an illness. Another takes a sugar pill, assuming it to be a potent drug. Both recover with equal speed. The expectation that the sugar pill will be therapeutic produces the cure. Indeed, "placebos" are acknowledged to be effective in twenty to forty percent of medical cases.

The influence of expectation on healing is age-old. In primitive cultures, local shamans often traded on faith and strong conviction, masquerading both beneath potions and symbols. What really cured was the unshakeable and absolute belief in the power of the magic. Conversely, belief in the negative symbol could have harmful effects. Walter Cannon of Harvard reported numerous cases of individuals who died only hours after a voodoo shaman put the curse on them. In the right context, expectation can produce extraordinary results.

But expectation has other less miraculous functions. It is helpful in planning for the future and eliminating surprise. It projects us into the next day or year so we are able to foresee what is required and respond accordingly. It provides a mental dress rehearsal of sorts which allows us to prepare for a variety of contingencies. Particularly in matters of security and survival, this is a matchless ability which to some extent explains our survival as a species. To a lesser degree, activities such as retirement planning, buying a smoke alarm, or saving money for our child's education demonstrate the value of expectation in preparing for the long haul.

Expectation also organizes our view of the world. We perceive in accordance with what we expect to see. This is because our anticipations set a context for how we will process new information. A photograph of a house cat inadvertently introduced by the photographer as a picture of a mountain lion will probably be interpreted in line with the viewer's expectation. Likewise, a vague shadow in a darkened room may be seen as a menacing figure if we are feeling fearful or vulnerable.

We see an extreme form of expectation's grip on perception in the individual with a paranoid disorder. He moves through life with the persistent and continued expectation that someone or something is out to get him. If offered food, he may think it poisoned. If given shelter, he may expect the room to be bugged. A pedestrian who looks askance at his queer behavior is judged as malevolent and a further sign of the conspiracy against him. All events are organized according to the delusional anticipation that the world will be hostile to him. To some extent the expectation is self-fulfilling, since his actions arouse discomfort and antipathy in others. But his continued madness is insured primarily by the flawed arrangement of his perceptions.

The Love Affair with Expectation

"And what wine is so sparkling, what so fragrant, what so intoxicating, as possibility." The Danish philosopher Kierkegaard wrote these words 150 years ago to describe the love affair human beings carry on with expectation. We love to "look forward to." We love to contemplate tomorrow. Sometimes we miss sleep thinking about the events of the next day. Other times we fantasize about the coming reunion with old friends or our rendezvous with a new lover. We relish expectation because thinking about events brings them to present consciousness and gives us a delightful taste of what is to come. Expectation builds excitement. We commonly use it to raise the level of desire. It is the force that transforms ordinary wish into yearning. In this sense it exists in the service of passion, a special form of aphrodisiac, concocted by the imagination of possibility. Consider these examples:

A young child is going to the circus for the first time. Her mind races with the thoughts and images she has associated with the Big Top. She contemplates coming face to face with lions and tigers, clowns and trapeze artists. She replays these images in her mind until she can barely contain her excitement.

A studious eighteen-year-old is preparing for her first year of college. She daydreams about living on her own, the stimulating classes, and the formation of new friendships. She particularly enjoys imagining literature courses where she sees herself in an erudite dialogue with her professors discussing the great writers Dostoevski, Shakespeare, Blake. Anticipation of these exchanges creates feelings of pure delight within her. She experiences herself as very adult and wise.

A former college athlete has joined a weekend softball team. Although she has not played in fifteen years, in her mind she pictures herself moving with grace and skill as she fields groundballs and picks off line drives. She envisions hitting home runs and trotting around the bases to the cheers of the crowd. She meditates on these glorious expectations, increasing her desire to get out and play.

In each situation, imagining possibility builds excitement and generates energy. The child, student, and former athlete draw on past experience, association, and fantasy to create a thought picture of what is to come. These images—whether fact or fancy—stimulate desire and send a tremor of exhilaration through the mind and body. They create aliveness and stir the blood. They sharpen the senses and increase delight with the future. Samuel Johnson said it well: "We love to expect, and when expectation is either disappointed or gratified, we want to be again expecting."

Negative Expectation

There are really two kinds of expectation: positive and negative, each reflecting how we envision what is to come. On the one hand, positive expectation results in disappointment when it goes unmet. On the other, failed negative expectation brings relief and sometimes unbridled joy.

All positive expectation contains an assessment and a wish for a certain course of events. "I expect to have a good time" means "I want to" and "In all probability I will." Negative expectation contains an assessment and a fear. "I expect she won't love me" equals "In all likelihood she won't" and "I'm afraid she won't." Negative expectations are always defensive in character. Historically, our first expectations are exclusively positive, strongly embodying our wishes. But as we grow up and in the process experience disappointment, we develop negative expectations, mostly as a way to protect ourselves from being let down. "I expect she won't love me" is really a maneuver to protect against failure of the wish "I want her to love me."

Negative expectations mirror our fears, especially those dreaded thoughts that our wishes will go ungratified. We will measure the effectiveness of this sort of disappointment defense later in the chapter.

what happens when you are waiting for a negative expectation but the outcome is positive?

The Other Side of the Story

The very aspects of expectation that benefit us also work to our disadvantage. When we anticipate an event, we create a mental set on the future. That is, we program our minds to notice only the things we expect to see. In doing so, we limit what we can take in. Our expectation acts as a kind of screen to other stimuli. An old Yiddish folktale demonstrates this point.

A seeker travels hundreds of miles on foot through natural and man-made adversity to learn the mysteries of life from a renowned *tsaddik*. After much misadventure he arrives exhausted in the tiny village and inquires where he can find the famous sage whose reputation is known far and wide.

Given directions, he proceeds to a small hovel where he encounters an old man dressed in rags, as unkempt as a beggar and obviously very poor.

Startled that a man of such wisdom could appear so wretched but not wishing to offend him, the seeker introduces himself, identifies his mission, and sits down. The old man immediately sets before him a meal of wine and cheese.

The seeker, still disturbed by the old man's appearance and living conditions, can barely contain himself and blurts out, "How can such a thing be? I did not expect this at all!"

To which the sage calmly replies, "What, you were expecting maybe herring with sour cream?"

The story tells how expectation can get in one's way. The seeker expected someone grander and more pretentious than the figure in rags standing before him. He has trouble adjusting to the new circumstances. The sage, at ease with himself, chooses not to acknowledge the man's disappointment in his appearance. Instead, he trivializes the man's reaction. It is as if he were saying, "What you expected me to look like is of no consequence. Don't let your lost expectation deter you from your real mission!"

Expectations—met or unmet—draw our attention away from other, sometimes more important perceptions. We have the capacity to be so engrossed in our anticipations that like the seeker we are distracted from what is in front of our nose. Expecting to see an airplane in the night sky, we miss the shooting star or, for that matter, don't notice that someone is picking our pocket. Expectation has the power to limit as well as enhance the experience. A male friend, a teacher in his early thirties, struggled for a number of years over whether to marry a particular woman. In many ways, she was a wonderful life partner for him. They shared mutual interests, enjoyed each other's company, dealt well with conflict, loved and respected one another. My friend was troubled, however, by this woman's past. She had been a topless dancer for a brief period in her life, and with his strict religious background he would not tolerate this one flaw. He expected the woman he married to be as pure as Sierra snow, and his continued focus on this minor event distracted him from the sensational woman she in fact was. His expectation—and his subsequent disappointment in her—limited his vision. He could only see the imperfections in the diamond. The beauty and luster were lost to him.

As we already know, expecting helps to eliminate the threat or discomfort associated with surprise. Anticipation can be thought of as mental preparation, and we can hardly be startled if we are prepared. But the cost of living with a future that is predictable can be exorbitant. When all events are anticipated, we lose our sense of adventure. We do not permit life to unfold before us, or respond to events as they come. As much as expectation may increase excitement, it also has the equal facility to make things too safe, too predictable. Boredom and caution travel the same road.

For all its advantage, expectation can feel like a burden. When we hold impossibly high standards for our behavior, we create the preconditions for disappointment in self. More than that, we make life ponderous and exhausting, since we are always trying to live up to a level of perfection that is unattainable. Some people believe that without high expectations they would be slothful or indolent. They assume the only thing that keeps them on track is their internal requirement for excellence. Such people are genuinely unhappy because they are unwilling to accept themselves for all that they are—good and bad, outstanding and mediocre.

Likewise, when we assume an obligation to fulfill the expectations of important people around us—our spouses, parents, teachers—we generally feel encumbered. We do it in order to win their favor, avoid disapproval, and gain increased self-esteem. But attending to the real or imagined agenda of others creates a situation in which we lose sight of our own desires and needs. Our sense of identity is never allowed full expression, and eventually we're left resentfully seeking a way to live expectation-free.

Clearly, expectations can be helpful allies or dreaded foes. A great deal depends on how deeply we invest in them and how much we identify them with ourselves. If we look at the current popular notions regarding expectation, three approaches stand out. Each offers a flawed remedy for the elimination of disappointment.

The All-Positive Approach

This notion is rooted in the one-sided view that if we expect good things for ourselves—indeed, envision them actively—they will come to pass. Code phrases: "Think positively"; "You create tomorrow"; "Expect to get what you want and you will." Such thinking suggests that expectation psychologically prepares the individual for success and eliminates negative self-fulfilling ideas. The formula runs something like this: Expecting success leads to thinking successfully, which leads to acting successfully, which eventually leads to being successful. There is some truth in this proposition. As we know, believing in yourself and setting your sights on what you want can have salutary effects. The athlete who does not believe he will win the race is unlikely to do so. The sales executive who is certain she will close the deal is more likely to accomplish the feat than a doubting competitor.

As an overall approach to expectation, however, this Pollyannaish view is incomplete and misleading. For one thing, it offers no qualifications and no limits, implying that expecting anything long and hard enough will produce the desired result. This is nothing more than wishful thinking presented in the guise of enlightened consciousness. Expectation itself rarely challenges the boundaries of reality except under the strictest of conditions. Believing in fairies just won't keep Tinker Bell alive.

Unconditional positive expectations create the climatic conditions for a bumper crop of disappointment, particularly if one's expectations are improbable and unattainable. The power of positive thinking offers no guarantees. The consequence of its failure is disappointment. To many, therefore, this perspective is viewed as a blueprint for disillusionment. As one of my patients remarked, "Each time I tried using 'positive affirmations' and was unsuccessful, I was reminded of how far I was from my goals. In a way, it provoked more disappointment!"

It is also perilous to apply our positive expectations to other people. What may be considered a harmless, well-intentioned expectation for one's spouse may be experienced by the other as an unwanted burden.

The all-positive approach is a rather fanciful new-age sleight of hand that answers our wishes for the world to be exactly as we desire it. It says to us, "You don't have to accept the pain of life. Think positively, act positively, and your world will be transformed." Such an optimistic view cannot help but attract us. Yet it denies the real character of existence with its pleasure *and* pain, despair as well as joy. No one is immune from the slings and arrows of outrageous fortune. Writer-philosopher Sam Keen writes convincingly:

> Life is not a bowl of Librium. And a good part of the secret of happiness lies in learning to suffer with dignity. Loneliness, loss, disappointment, failure, disease, boredom are inevitable. The price of trying to avoid the unavoidable is illusion, or neurosis. Even if you jog, eat health foods, grow, meditate, and go to confession regularly you will sometimes fall sick... Your best-laid plans won't coerce the future. Nothing you can do will keep those you love from dying. You can never be fully safe. The fears of abandonment and annihilation are in the DNA. They are the Siamese twin of the will to live.

The Doomsday Approach

This popular, rather cynical viewpoint may be stated in this way: "Expect the worst and you will never be disappointed or hurt." Code phrases: "What do you expect?"; "Be prepared for the worst"; "Only fools are satisfied." The approach represents a 180-degree shift from the all-positive position. It relies exclusively on negative expectation. If things work out better than anticipated, so much the better. As we know, such stratagems are distinctly defensive. Only an individual who has been deeply disappointed would subscribe to them as a form of insurance against future pain. But there is a deep illogic and underlying despair to the viewpoint. It is somewhat akin to smashing your kneecaps with a hammer just to feel the exquisite sense of relief when the pain subsides. The experience of expecting the worst brings with it pessimism and gloominess that masquerade as wisdom but are themselves toxic. The solution is worse than the problem.

Just as positive expectations are self-fulfilling to some degree, negative expectations can be too. People who expect unpleasantness set themselves up through their negativity to receive it. Like flypaper to the fly, they seem to attract calamity. The ballplayer who expects to drop the flyball usually fails to make the catch. The job hunter who expects to do poorly on the interview most often does. Negative expectation can create negative experience which, in turn, reinforces the belief that low expectation is justifiable. And so the doomsday cycle is perpetuated.

Of course, negative expectation is sometimes justifiable and realistic. Some patients I have seen, for example, have been reared by parents who have severe emotional problems and are incapable of loving their offspring. In such circumstances, the negative expectation "I won't get what I want from Mother" is entirely appropriate and, in fact, a correct assessment of reality. But every situation does not require a negative appraisal. As an approach to expectation, the doomsday notion is highly unsuccessful because it helps create the very situation of disappointment it is attempting to combat.

The Eradication Approach

Put simply, this view would have us live without expectation. By anticipating nothing and accepting events as they come, disappointment would be eliminated. The formula is straightforward: no expectation, no disappointment. If we don't expect to be secretary of state, president of the corporation, or treasurer of the PTA, we will not feel bad when we don't make it. Code phrases: "Be spontaneous"; "Live in the moment"; "Take each day as it comes." As I noted in Chapter Two, there is merit in the idea of permanent present-centeredness, of living in the "here and now" without preconceived notions of what we want from the future. All the problems caused by expectation would be eliminated if we could rid ourselves of the expectation habit. But can we? And what do we lose in the process?

We lose a great deal. The capacity to expect adds a richness to our lives that cannot be overlooked or discounted. Without it, we reduce the level of excitation and passion, forego planning and organizing functions, lessen our motivation and with it our hopes for the future. The forfeit of expectation results in an impoverishment of our lives that can only be compared to the sacrifice of imagination or the ability to dream great dreams. Those who advocate the eradication of expectation are sometimes the same individuals who have suffered such serious disappointment that they are afraid of ever wanting anything strongly again. One of my patients was a dancer who, after years of preparing for her career, suffered an injury to her knee that left her unable to continue. Her disappointment was monumental. She saw her whole life as preparation for a journey that was now impossible to take. Dismayed and despairing, she defended against similar circumstances by not allowing herself any intense desire. She became blasé and indifferent, almost frozen in her rigid defense. Only by risking "wanting" again was she able to overcome her despair.

Even if we are willing to eliminate desire (the cause of all suffering, according to Buddha), the question remains as to whether human beings are capable of such an adjustment over the long haul. Perhaps in the confines of a time-limited vacation, a protected environment, or in a defensive paralysis, yes, but it is unrealistic to believe that in modern life— with all its stress and complexity—we can live without expectations. It would require superhuman discipline and energy, and a level of perfection that is uncharacteristic of the species. The eradication approach is really a utopian vision of life without general applicability to large numbers of people. The best that we can hope for is a reduction in the level of expectation. Elimination is virtually impossible. Like fear of abandonment or annihilation, it is built into the DNA.

Preventing Chronic Disappointment

Since all these popular notions of expectation are blemished or deficient, we need to develop another perspective that is more sensible for preventing and minimizing chronic disappointment. Bear in mind that expectation itself is not the problem. It is our relationship to expectation that needs modification. We are too invested in expecting, too stubborn in relinquishing what cannot come to pass. Disappointment is a function of this obstinacy.

It is always a dangerous business to advocate a particular psychological solution to a problem as thorny and recurrent as disappointment. To do so is to oversimplify the issues involved and risk excluding those whose unique situations do not seem relevant. Worse, there is the danger of setting up unrealistic expectations. We already know the consequences of that action.

With these concerns in mind I am putting forth seven basic principles (not a formula) which, carefully followed, will reduce chronic disappointment in most situations. I do not say "eliminate," for that task is truly impossible. In life, disappointment is inevitable and also of value in shaping our world view and helping us to fathom possibility (more on this in Chapter Twelve).

Two notions are essential to our task. First, the attitude we hold toward expectation is critical. Second, the degree of realism reflected in our expectations determines whether they succeed or fail, and hence how disappointed we are.

Seven Principles to Reduce Disappointment

Maintain a Flexible Attitude

The first step in forming a new, disappointment-free relationship with expectation is to maintain a more flexible attitude. Keep perspective on your expectations. Be prepared to change them when circumstances indicate they're unlikely to be met. Don't invest too heavily in any one outcome.

Keep Perspective: Approach expectations without reverence or attachment. No expectations are sacrosanct. Few involve matters of life and death. And none are irreplaceable. As important as expectation in general may be in helping us to function in the world, no *single* hoped-for outcome is essential. Remember that expectations are nothing more than wish and anticipation. Don't empower them with the twin illusions of necessity or indispensability. Don't give them royal treatment or see them as permanent fixtures that cannot be removed or changed without great pain. Think of them as dessert, delicious and tempting but not obligatory. Expectations are helpful and pleasurable only if we see them clearly without overvaluing them.

Be Prepared to Change: A key to reducing disappointment is a willingness to give up what you want when you can't get it. Consider the situation of a man who is disappointed that his new car is not getting superior gas mileage despite repeated trips to the mechanic. A chronic disappointment sufferer would continue to expect an unrealistic forty-miles-to-the-gallon, and every visit to the gas pump would be cause for annoyance and regret. A disappointment-free individual would either give up the expectation and accept the less-than-desired mileage or get rid of the car. His approach is characterized by a clear reading of the situation and adaptability if events do not go as anticipated. Those who are able to adjust to the contingencies of unexpected circumstances don't get let down. They get satisfied.

Reduce Your Investment: We are overly invested in particular expectations. As a result, we hold onto them long after it is advisable, suffering disappointment in the process. We need to reduce and sometimes liquidate our investment. The problem is not so much in the intensity of what we expect but in the degree of attachment. And it is precisely where we find it hardest to disengage that we have the greatest investment. We have come to identify with our expectations as if they were a measure of ourselves. The woman who hopes to rise one day to the top of the corporate structure would look unfavorably on relinquishing her expectation. Perhaps she relies on it for motivation, but we can be equally certain she sees it as a measure of her worth. She defines the level of her capability by the quality of her vision. Dreaming great dreams reflects well on the dreamer. And if she cannot achieve her expectation, she can at least separate herself from the herd by anticipating a wondrous future.

Although we may enjoy associating ourselves with great expectations, what we *do* in reality is a far better criterion of individual merit than what we expect. Even the ne'er-do-well may envision a life of fame and fortune. In identifying with our expectations, we give them an authority and urgency which they do not truly deserve. To maintain a flexible attitude we need to remember that we are *not* our expectations. They do not define us any more than our shoe size does. Surrendering them is not the same as surrendering self. Indeed, as individual egos, we continue to exist long after we give up the desire for a particular outcome.

The most convincing explanation as to why we invest in our expectations so fervently is that they express our hopes and wishes for ourselves, others, and the world. Wishes are the middle ground between what we see and what we expect. In the words of psychoanalysis, they are pure "pleasure principle." It is really the wish below each expectation to which we are betrothed. And it is the deeper lifewish—for the world to be just, without frustration, and so forth—to which we are married.

To give up our attachment to an expectation, we must be willing to divorce the wish, a step few people are willing to take without prompting. We can hide in our wishes from the way things really are. "I wish the accident hadn't happened." "I wish I had won the game." Ultimately, reducing our attachment to expectation means a willingness to accept the negative aspects of life and give up our wishes and illusions about how we would like it to be.

Trim Down Expectations—Know What You Want

It would take you and your calculator several minutes to add up the number of daily expectations held by the average individual. In the first fifteen minutes of the day we have already expected the alarm clock to sound, the toothpaste to be where we left it, the toaster to evenly brown the bread, even the car to start on demand. The list of trivial expectations is endless. Most are hardly worth a second thought, except when things don't go right!

Beyond the trivial, though, most people carry around too many expectations, particularly in the important areas of sex, relationship, work, and family. We have already seen how in these times—with the breakdown of familiar sex roles— it is not uncommon to expect one's spouse to be all things— from lover to business partner. The burden of such expectation is a significant load to bear. No one's shoulders are wide enough, and many relationships fail as a consequence of the disappointment and resentment that necessarily follow. Likewise, we expect a great deal more from work than in previous generations. We want to identify ourselves with our livelihood and draw esteem and power as well as money from it. Given the number of jobs and the corporate emphasis on profit, these expectations are simply too unrealistic to be met in every case. Many will be disappointed. Sexuality has been trivialized by an overabundance of statistics, gadgetry, and orgasmic curve charts. We now commonly accept our "right" to satisfaction, and pity the lover who does not respect it! Instead of the roguish lothario of two decades ago, we expect a partner to be sensitive, nurturing, exciting, communicative, willing, and sexually knowledgeable. Surely we have set the stage for disillusionment among the actors in this drama.

To prevent disappointment, we must reduce the sheer number of expectations that we hold and scale them down to meet the realities of current life. Perhaps André Gide was right when he said, "Long only for what you have." But no one wants to hear this sort of message. It runs counter to an important American myth: Any size dream can come true with enough determination and elbow grease. Many a politician has been forced into early retirement for advocating that we lower our expectations to reflect greater realism.

The deeper psychological truth is that our expectations are often confused or poorly conceived. When we don't really know what we want, we entertain all sorts of desires in the hope of finding that one object or situation that will bring satisfaction. We operate under the misconception that fulfillment of large numbers of wants and expectations is correlated with happiness. The fulfillment of a dozen needless expectations, however, merely results in more disappointment and confusion when we feel no better: "Why don't these things make me happy?"

Define your expectations carefully. Sometimes we pursue what we "should" or "ought to," not what is genuinely satisfying or fitting. Other times we hold ideal expectations for ourselves which are either impossible to attain or simply unsuited to our level of skill and ability. We would like to be a distinguished professor, a professional athlete, an internationally known opera star, but are our talents and natural endowments equal to the task?

To avoid disappointment in self, our expectations should be realistic and based on a practical assessment of our capabilities. Know what you can do and pursue it. Expect of yourself only what you are capable of achieving and what you really want. What expectations are yours by conscious choice as opposed to those learned automatically at your parent's knee?

When expectations are trimmed down to a manageable number and are based on an honest—not an ideal—assessment of what we really want for ourselves and others, the preconditions for disappointment are reduced.

Develop Second-Order Expectations

Suppose I meet a married couple to whom I take an immediate liking. Not only do we share common interests and preferences, but we have all grown up in similar circumstances. Our early histories are an initial bond, and we decide to get to know each other better. We plan a quiet weekend in the mountains at a small country inn. I have high expectations. I hope to deepen our relationship, but the weekend does not go as planned. I don't get along with my new friends. She seems hostile, he is withdrawn. They treat each other without any affection or respect and all they talk about is money. Our conversations are trivial and dull. They don't appear anxious to connect with me. Having limited choices, I manage the weekend as best I can and part amicably but with some relief.

I'm disappointed. I wanted things to go differently. I had hoped to develop a lasting friendship. Over the next week, however, my disappointment begins to fade, and I blame my experience on other factors: the poor food at the inn, the soft beds that prevented a good night's sleep, the flat tire on the drive up, the absence of a deck of playing cards. By the following weekend I have managed to deny altogether my uncomfortable feelings toward my new friends. In six weeks time, when they suggest we take another weekend trip together, I agree. You might guess the outcome—again!

The problem is that I didn't learn from my initial experience. I denied my feelings, pretended other factors ruined the trip, and consequently made the same error twice. As awful as disappointment may feel, it has a good deal to teach us about the limits of reality. I just wasn't paying enough attention to take my lessons seriously.

My original expectations were to get to know my new friends better and to enjoy myself in the process. These are what I call first-order expectations. They are pure, rather innocent, and largely wishful anticipations that are felt in circumstances not previously encountered. They are untested by experience, having never been gratified or dashed. Of course, if I had more carefully assessed the situation and taken a keener look at this couple, I might have known better. Instead I allowed my wish to make new friends over-

whelm any critical assessment. In truth, I was more hopeful
than perceptive. But anyone can make a mistake. We all act
unconsciously at times. Once disappointed, however, I have
a much clearer choice. I can deny my experience, learn
nothing from it, and be vulnerable to a repeat performance.
Or I can create a second-order expectation, a new response
based on a better assessment of reality. After all, no one is
in a better position to form an enlightened expectation than
an individual who has already experienced the situation. A
second-order expectation is an educated anticipation built
on the ruins of previous disappointment. It reflects a veteran
knowledge of possibility gathered from an episode of failed
expectation. Let us see what sort of second-order expectations I might have developed after the initial disappointing
weekend. My first-order expectations were obviously unrealistic. Now that I know the couple better, I see that I
really don't like them. What's more, they aren't particularly
interested in me. So what can I practically expect? Three
new expectations are appropriate:

1. I no longer expect them to become my good friends.
2. I expect to limit my investment in a future relation-
    ship with them.
3. I expect to temper my hopes for new friends with
    caution.

Had I created these second-order expectations after the
first weekend, I would have spared myself additional disappointment.

Because we are interested in burying discomfort as quickly
as possible, we don't always learn from our failed expectations. We avoid the disappointment by moving on to other

things. Or we are so pained by our loss that we remain stuck in the disappointment experience and cannot assess the situation clearly. Either way we lose out.

We need to develop and enlarge second-order expectation. More than any single action, this process will bring results in preventing recurring disillusionment. All of us have been disappointed enough in life to have acquired the knowledge to virtually eliminate habitual patterns. We have only to search our memories. If this suggestion seems difficult, use the exercise below to help you dig out past hurts. You'll need a comfortable chair, paper and pencil, and about fifteen minutes of quiet time.

1. Relax for ten minutes, breathing fully and regularly into your abdomen and chest.

2. Close your eyes. Count down (in your head) from ten to one. With each number allow yourself to relax more deeply.

3. Remember five significant disappointments from your life. Take your time. Don't try hard, just let the incidents enter your consciousness. When you recall each, raise your index finger in the air about forty-five degrees. As you lower your finger, let yourself experience the feelings associated with each disappointment.

4. Now open your eyes and write down on a sheet of paper your failed·expectations for each incident.

5. Ask yourself, "What does each disappointment tell me about what I can realistically expect the next time?"

6. Create a second-order expectation that reflects this knowledge.

7. Note that second-order expectations can be both positive and negative: "I expect..." as well as "I no longer expect..." Keep a balance between these two possibilities.

Too much negative expectation has a defensive quality. Positive formulations are more affirmative and satisfying.

Use More Assessment, Less Wish

Another way of preventing disappointment is to change the nature of first-order expectations. As I noted earlier, every positive expectation—regardless of which order—combines both a wish and an assessment of possibility. "I expect to get the job" means both "I am looking forward to being hired" and "I will likely be hired." When the relationship between these components is askew, we create the preconditions for letdown. Chronically disappointed individuals not only fail to develop second-order expectations, they also put too much wish and too little assessment in their first-order expectations. They are overly influenced by desire and not heedful of probability. Like children, what they anticipate is synonymous with what they want. Consequently, their expectations are unrealistic and often fail.

The remedy? Put more assessment into first-order expectation. Take out or diminish the wish component. This action requires an awareness of what you really expect as well as frequent reevaluation. Whenever you are approaching a new situation, it is helpful to know clearly and precisely beforehand what your expectations are. Once you have this knowledge, you can assess their possibility on the Attainability Continuum. Remember, in weighing the realism of an expectation, you must not only ask, "Is it possible?" but also "Is it possible in this particular situation?" Attainability is a function of both expectation and context. The Continuum allows us to graphically represent how realistic our expectations are. It introduces a rational perspective to counteract the wish component in our view of the future.

Eliminate Absolute and Exacting Expectations

Although we may choose to hide the fact from ourselves, many expectations are so exacting or absolute that their satisfaction is virtually impossible to achieve. For example, I may expect my spouse to be cheerful and attentive whenever I arrive home; my life to be a model of productivity and efficiency; my friends to be available whenever I need them. At first glance, none of these presumptions seems patently unreasonable because we assume that an occasional violation will be tolerated, chalked up to human fallibility. However, when expectations are imbued with symbolic meaning or the person holding them requires perfection, deviation is not acceptable. One hundred percent compliance is truly desired and fully expected. If a spouse is not attentive at every homecoming or if life is not always productive, disappointment is the consequence.

Many individuals who feel repeated disappointment tend to formulate absolute expectations. They use words such as "always," "never," and "every." Others, despite the qualified language of their expectations, act as if they were indeed absolute. "I expect you to be home most of the time" may imply, "I expect you to be home *all* the time." Since human beings are fallible, those who demand faultlessness are usually disappointed. "Why can't people act as responsibly as I do?" is their usual refrain. They operate under the misconception that absolute expectations bring out the best in themselves and others. Social research indicates this thinking is erroneous. Setting rigidly high standards rarely results in optimal performance, and most people react to the burden of impossible expectations with resentment.

Consider your own expectations. Are they absolute and overly demanding? Do you expect your children *always* to reflect well on you, or that every sexual experience must be wonderfully satisfying? To prevent disappointment, we need to eliminate unconditional and peremptory expectations and substitute less narrow and more tolerant requirements for satisfaction. Suppose we go to a play and the principal actor—whom we have always enjoyed—is out with a cold. Nevertheless, the performance is excellent. Are we disappointed or satisfied? If our expectations were defined absolutely, we will go home disappointed. But if our expectations are broader and more loosely constructed, we will feel satisfaction since the play itself was enjoyable. Or perhaps we expect our sexual partner to be "attractive." A great deal depends on how rigidly we define that adjective. Does he have to look like Paul Newman or will a reasonably healthy and well-cared-for individual fit the bill? Exacting and idealized expectations make gratification that much more difficult. The less absolute the expectation, the greater its chance for its success.

Expect Some Disappointment

It is important to remember that *some* disappointment is going to occur no matter how judicious you may be. Provide for this possibility in your life so that you are prepared for occasional letdown. Such precaution is not the same as adopting negative expectations, but it does acknowledge the capricious nature of disappointment and the lack of certainty in daily living. There is no fail-safe method for preventing disappointment. The wish to eradicate it completely like some household pest is yet another unrealistic expectation that produces the very condition it purports to avoid.

Maintain Hope

As we pare down our expectations, eliminating the unnecessary, unrealistic, and absolute, we may find ourselves wondering how we will face tomorrow without the lifewishes and dreams that underlie our expectancies. What is the consequence of starting a relationship without any preconceptions or interviewing for a job without an overriding attachment to getting it. We cannot know with certainty until we experiment with this new perspective.

In reducing expectations we are eliminating particular wishes and dreams, but we do not have to discard the attitude of hope along with them. We can maintain it without investing in specific hopes.

Hope, in the singular, is an outlook, a perspective on the future that cannot be destroyed by a single loss. It is larger than our attachments. Lifewishes may come and go but hope remains—a statement that we believe in tomorrow.

Chronic disappointment is the natural enemy of hope. The repeated experience of expecting and not receiving wears us down emotionally, erodes our optimism, and depletes our trust that circumstances will ever improve.

Ultimately, to live without habitual disappointment we must give up specific hopes but not the attitude of hoping. We must keep a vision of possibility without expecting it.

Thus we look forward to the future, but we keep our expectations for new relationship, job, or vacation, as close to zero as possible. This requires from each of us a certain amount of mental discipline and an element of faith that life will turn out all right even if events do not go as we expected.

CHAPTER 11

Up from Disappointment

The greatest discovery of any generation is that human beings can alter their lives by altering their attitudes of mind.
Albert Schweitzer

Although few people want to experience disappointment, many are fascinated by it. Literature abounds with classic stories of disappointed dreams and unrealized hopes. From Madame Bovary to Anna Karenina, Hamlet to Heathcliff, the drawing rooms, bedchambers, and misty moors of countless dramas hang heavy with despair and rude awakenings. None of those works is more graphic than the contemporary play *Death of a Salesman*. In it, playwright Arthur Miller exposes the power of disappointment to undermine, corrupt, and finally destroy the lives of an American family. It is a tragic portrait of the common man, one Willy Loman, salesman, father, and husband, disillusioned with life and himself but unable to face his failures. To escape his disappointment, he mythologizes his success. But his talk is idle crowing. Willy has struggled all his life just to make ends meet. He is still a salesman after so many years, still driving the same lonely roads, selling undistinguished goods.

229

Recognizing his failures and changing his future is not in Willy's character. To escape the nagging truth, he directs his disappointment away from himself and onto his oldest son. Biff, a "golden boy" during childhood, has—like his father—failed to live up to the expected promise. At thirty-four he is still in search of himself, confused and unhappy. Contemptuous of his father, whom he had idolized until a traumatic incident in adolescence, he is impatient with Willy's self-deception. Ultimately these emotions poison the entire Loman family and force Willy into a desperate act of self-justification. He takes his own life so that his family will receive money from his insurance policy.

Death of a Salesman is a story about the ravages of disappointment. Willy hides from his dashed expectations by denying their failure. To the end, he is a man who misses the obvious. His wishes blur his vision and inevitably ruin him. Dreams are the last refuge of the disappointed, but the price of living through them is high. As the philosopher Thomas Hobbes reminds us, "Men are sometimes free to do what they wish, but they are never free in their wishes."

There are many lessons contained in this tragedy. One message is fundamental. The denial of disappointment is the gravest of errors. It leads us to a far greater desperation in the long run and prevents us from addressing the unrealistic expectations on which our feelings are based. Willy pretended he had made it big. Everyone else recognized his charade but chose to protect him from himself. They colluded in the deceit which eventually brought the man down.

Moving out of disappointment begins with a recognition of one's feelings of loss. This is step one. We cannot hope for improvement without acknowledging our dilemma and our need to change. Like Willy Loman, a surprisingly large number of individuals block awareness of their disappointment. They feel vague signs of distress: a depressive malaise, a loss of excitement, a nagging sense of defeat. But they don't attach these signals to any particular cause. Perhaps they are avoiding the self-evident, hoping it will go away like a sudden stomach pain or a pang of self-doubt. Maybe they see it as a Pandora's box that, once opened, will cause overwhelming problems. While investigating the levels of disappointment in our culture, I discovered a curious fact. In opinion polls, which base their findings entirely on self-report, respondents tend to express high rates of personal satisfaction for themselves, but perceive lower rates for others. In a 1978 *Better Homes and Gardens* survey on the family, for example, seventy-six percent of those polled believed family life in America was in trouble, while eighty-five percent of the same group reported that most of their expectations of happiness in marriage had been fulfilled.

Could it be that we just don't like to admit to our own problems although we can easily detect them in our neighbors? Or are we projecting our troubles onto others while refusing to own up to them ourselves? Becoming aware of our difficulties forces us to decide whether to exert effort to change and possibly risk greater hazards or to do nothing and passively accept the current undesirable circumstances. By keeping up the illusion of happiness or projecting dissatisfaction onto others, we avoid consciousness of this unwelcome choice.

Disappointment and Change

Since the journey up from disappointment involves the very same principles as any personal change, the more we know about change the better. As you would expect, individuals who have difficulty making any sort of significant modification in their lives also have problems moving out of disappointment. One might call these chronically disillusioned individuals "change-phobic." They fear the unpredictability associated with new circumstance. They prefer to remain uncomfortably disappointed rather than risk attempting what is unfamiliar and therefore threatening.

What does psychology have to offer us as we try to understand the change process? Unfortunately, it does not provide a unified view. Behaviorists contend that all change is a simple matter of reinforcement. Rewarded actions are repeated. Unrewarded or negatively rewarded behavior is extinguished. The noted psychologist B. F. Skinner claims, "A person does not act upon the world, the world acts upon him." This view is different from the psychoanalytic perspective, which we might call deterministic. According to Freud, our actions are governed by internal forces over which we have limited control. Life is lived with only the illusion of choice. The unconscious is the real governing body.

In bold contrast, the humanist and existential psychologies maintain that human beings have free will and individuals are the architects of their own lives, not only in what they choose to do but in how they choose to experience it. They emphasize that although circumstances may be limited by chance, genetics, or environment—what philosopher Jean-Paul Sartre calls the "coefficient of adversity"—our attitudes toward life determine our experience. Even in the face of death, we can control how we leave this earth—with a grimace or an uproarious laugh.

Few of us would accept the notion that character is set by the first three years of life, as Freud would have us believe. Or that we are walking computers, responding blindly and predictably to reward and punishment—the behaviorist approach. With the threat of nuclear annihilation looming over us, neither can we embrace the existential principle of absolute free will. We are pawns in a larger game. As it stands, none of the three viewpoints are entirely satisfying. Yet, as veterans of life, we know we have the power to influence at least our immediate circumstances. We also, in turn, are influenced by them. We operate in a reciprocal arrangement. Sometimes we create change, other times we are the objects of change. We are both the creator and the creation.

The ability to make personal change hinges initially on a single question: "Does the power to alter my life originate in me?" (Can I stop being disappointed?) The question is important because without the belief that one's destiny is at least partially self-determined, the ballgame is over. Fatalists who view themselves as just so many autumn leaves blown by the winds of fortune have neither the motivation nor the faith to take control over their lives. They see all action as futile since the locus of control is outside themselves. Their position is self-fulfilling. The woman who declares: "I have a bad temper; it's just the way I am!" has elected to maintain a specific relationship to her anger. This attitude relieves her of the burden of change but undermines her connection with others. In the long run, she is injured by her own passivity. In order to change, we must believe in the notion that we can have an impact on our situation, that we are the authors of our actions and beliefs. This is what Sartre called "responsibility"—to be "the uncontested author of an event or thing."

Four Steps to Change

Let us consider four separate factors needed to accomplish personal, volitional change: awareness, motivation, decision, action.

Awareness

We have already reflected on the necessity of awareness as the first step in making change. We must recognize our condition before we can alter it. A tumor unnoticed will go untreated. An unrecognized conflict between lovers will undermine the reservoir of accumulated, positive feeling. Awareness precedes all action.

Motivation

In order to make personal change we must have motivation—incentive that prompts us to act. Sometimes motivation is powerful and focused. When you burn your fingertips on a match, the desire to change your relationship to the matchstick is immediate and unfaltering. Other times motivation is indecisive or conflicting. You are uncertain whether to go to a party. You'd like to make some new friends but feel tired and unsociable.

We may be motivated by reason and insight, as the philosophers Descartes, Hobbes, and Spinoza nobly assumed. Or we may be inspired by hedonism, a movement toward pleasure and away from pain. Instinctive drives such as sex, hunger, and aggression incline us to action. So do a wide range of emotions from fear to jealousy. Even social motives for approval, conformity, and relatedness can arouse us. Motivation is a complex, internal process that may involve more than one compelling drive. The professor who prepares all day for a lecture may be prompted by many concerns. He may wish simultaneously to communicate information, win the esteem of his students, and escape from a bad marriage. And he himself may be unaware of the third factor. We are not always cognizant of every motive, regardless of how obvious it may be to others.

Decision

Psychologists have endlessly debated whether we must actually move through the experience of decision before change is made. Many contend that since decision—or the commitment to action—is impossible to measure through experimentation, we cannot rightfully assume it exists. Others contend that life is a process of continual decision-making and that our world view is constructed not only by what we choose but by what we perceive as our alternatives. Anyone who has ever struggled with the issues of how to raise a child, succeed at work, or overcome internal lethargy knows that deciding to take action is a basic part of making change. But the issue is not quite so simple. We make decisions in an active manner: I choose to go to the picnic, divorce my spouse, run for Congress. But we are equally capable of making them in passive fashion. By choosing not to choose, in effect we make a choice. For example, a runner is undecided about whether to participate in a New Year's Day marathon. By avoiding the decision she forfeits an active choice. Nonetheless, by January second, her ambivalence has been translated into decision. She has missed the race.

The absence of a conscious decision-process does not mean she has failed to choose. Indeed, some of the most important life decisions are regrettably made by passive abstention.

Facing change means facing risk. Will our new circumstances make us better off? Will we make a grave error? We cannot know with certainty unless we try the new course of action. For many people, personal change is too risky. They would rather wear a worn-out but familiar pair of shoes than try on a new one with all its potential problems. They worry that the new shoes may be too small, too stiff, or unattractive. Yet one must also consider the price of wearing the old pair for a lifetime. Sometimes change is needed to provide vitality and contrast. By enlivening us and sharpening our wits, risk can become our ally.

Action

Once we make a committed decision, the next step is to put it into action. As sincere as they may appear, questions about *how* to act are often reflections of ambivalence in the decision to change. "How to" has a way of becoming clearer when we are fully committed. In psychotherapy, many patients try to delay taking action by focusing on the details of change. One patient, who for years was unable to express his deep feelings of anger toward his critical, abusive father, insisted on creating an elaborate scheme of fail-safe contingencies. His meticulous preparations were really a means of avoiding the confrontation in the first place.

I often tell my patients that the action involved in change is the easiest aspect of the entire process. Finding the motivation and making the decision is where the internal battles are fought. Action is merely the follow-through in a process already set in motion.

Evading Change

Innumerable explanations may be given as to why people evade change. Some of these are specific to a particular situation, while others have relevance to a wide array of issues, including disappointment.

1. Every change involves contending with the unknown. The unknown is highly unpredictable and, therefore, filled with apprehension. The imagination's capacity to run wild upon entering a dark, unfamiliar room gives us some idea of how we can project catastrophic expectations onto new situations.

2. Each change creates an ending as well as a beginning. When we initiate a new course of action, we terminate at the same moment the old way of doing things. If we alter the way we relate to the boss, we discontinue the prior pattern of interaction. If we change an attitude or viewpoint, we surrender a former perspective. Thus every change necessarily produces the loss of the status quo. For many people, losing the familiar and the predictable is frightening. They would prefer painless change that did not require forsaking anything at all. Unfortunately, relinquishing established patterns is a prerequisite for any alteration in the way things are.

Situations in which what is given up is less valued than what is gained present the easiest transitions. Few people have difficulty adjusting to color television after black and white. On the other hand, circumstances in which what is lost is more attractive than what is gained discourage change. No one likes to think they are trading down.

3. Decision limits possibility. By choosing A, we exclude B. Each choice represents a path taken and a path rejected. Given

the opportunity, who would not prefer to have unlimited options? But possibility is endless as long as we don't act. Exclusion
begins as soon as we choose one thing over another. To decide
on a course of change produces this same exclusion.

4. Personal change is an experience of isolation. When we
alter the deep-rooted patterns of personality, we come face to
face with how alone we are in the world. Family and friends
may offer support, but they cannot create the change for us.
We go it alone and contend with the consequences essentially
by ourselves. The two most significant moments in the life
cycle—birth and death—are experienced alone.

5. Making change requires energy and commitment. Those
who live stressful lives do not relish additional pressure. They
are barely making it without introducing the effort required to
produce change. "Leave me alone," they complain. "It's difficult
enough to survive in this fast-paced, crazy world." But what
makes us think that life will be easier if we maintain a personal
status quo? Significant personal change allows us to deal more
effectively with the world by eliminating self-defeating and repetitive neurotic patterns. Ask anyone who has ever conquered
a phobia whether they are better off for having made the decision to challenge their anxieties.

6. Significant change often creates identity confusion. How
we view ourselves is supported by the life roles we play in work
and relationships as well as by our daily rituals and familiar
surroundings. Another way of saying this is that our sense of
identity is buttressed by the context in which we live. Take
away this context and the individual can feel as disoriented as
the proverbial fish out of water. I knew an important executive
who was much admired and respected by his colleagues. A
decision in midlife to change professions threw him into be-
wilderment and self-doubt. He was plagued with feelings of
inadequacy, and he questioned his previous success. Having
lost the validation of his peers and an ongoing role of importance, his identity had been undermined. It took him nearly a
year to come to grips with the questions raised by the job shift.

Many people avoid change because they are afraid of losing themselves in the change process.

The better you accommodate to new circumstances, the less disappointment you experience in life. Disappointed individuals have problems with change. They will do almost anything to avoid surrendering their old familiar shoes (expectations). With their toes exposed and their soles flapping, they insist on wearing their comfortable but ragged footgear.

In the Chinese language, the character used to indicate the word "crisis" has two meanings: danger and opportunity. Every disappointment is a crisis of sorts, and each allows us three opportunities. We can deny our feelings, pretend all is well, and hurt privately deep inside. We can also allow ourselves to feel disappointed, exaggerate the impact of our loss, and dwell on it. Or we can take an active role by accepting our disappointment and learning from it for the future. We always have a choice to act or to remain passive. What is your tendency? Do you sit back and bemoan your fate, or implement new approaches to the situation?

Tom's Story

The experience of Tom, a successful thirty-four-year-old management training director, provides us with an inside look at a crisis of disappointment that became an opportunity. After years of futile attempts to have a child, Tom learned what neither he nor his wife, Barbara, had initially suspected—that the problem originated with him. The results of a lab test showed that he was infertile and would never be able to father children. For a man who had rarely faced adversity, the news was jolting:

> I couldn't believe it! Here I was in the prime of my life, in great physical condition, with never so much as a cold, and the doctor was telling me I wasn't able to produce enough sperm to fertilize an egg. The idea was totally absurd. I could run twelve miles, chop a cord of wood, and play basketball for hours, but I couldn't produce enough sperm to create a kid. I remember feeling shaken and very defiant. I really couldn't accept it. Somehow, it didn't fit my image of myself.

Tom had always *expected* to father a child and raise a family. The knowledge that his goal was impossible angered and then embittered him. For some time, he refused to believe the diagnosis and demanded repeated verification. When he found conclusively that the sperm counts were accurate, he began to doubt himself. The idea of making a family was so fundamental to his world view that, when the possibility was removed, he wondered just who he was. He questioned his adequacy as a man and belittled his worth and desirability.

Months passed, but he still despaired over his great disappointment. His relationship with Barbara worsened. He always seemed to feel guilty around her. From his perspective, he had let her down and could find no adequate way to compensate her. His sexual interest waned, and he began to show signs of depression. He slept poorly and his interest in work declined.

At this point in the situation, Tom came to see me. He emphasized his wish to experience himself as a father, carrying on the family lineage. He wanted to sire a child who resembled him, "an image of myself in the next generation," is how he put it. He felt his circumstances to be terribly unfair. Why had this happened to him? He had never shown signs of physical abnormality. Perhaps the medical opinions were in error after all, and it would only be a matter of time before his wife became pregnant.

It was clear to me that Tom's predicament was a true crisis of disappointment. He expected to father a child. This goal was not biologically possible, however, and he was profoundly disillusioned. Stuck in the resistance and loss stages of the disappointment cycle, Tom's frustration fed on itself. It grew to such great proportions that it provoked identity questions, shaking the foundation of his self-image. As we tried to change this downward spiral of events, Tom and I had the following conversation:

Tom: I've been feeling very bad lately. This infertility business has worn me down and confused me. I don't know where I'm going or what I want. I never feel happy. In fact, I rarely feel anything at all. I used to have so much energy. Now I really don't care. It's hard to sort it all out. What's happening to me? I'm worried.

DB: Go back to the beginning. Where did it all start?

Tom: Well, I guess it began when I found out the lab test results. I couldn't believe what the doctor told me. I had thought the problem was my wife's, but as it turned out it was me that had the problem. I can't tell you how let down I felt. Nothing like this had ever happened to me before. I always got what I wanted. But not now.

DB: It's clear that disappointment is at the root of your problem. You didn't get something you really wanted and expected. What was it?

Tom: I expected to be a father. All my life, I've wanted a family. Sometimes I imagine carrying my child around with me in the neighborhood just so my friends would say, "Your kid's the spitting image of you, Tom." Isn't it an incredible thing to see yourself in the face of your two-year-old? But, of course, none of it's possible now.

DB: Your view of family life sounds rather sentimental and idealized. I'd like to know a little more about it.

Tom: I'm not sure what you mean. I want my own children, that's all. I can't imagine having a meaningful life without them. Why earn money if you can't give it to your children? Why struggle if it's not to make their lives easier? Damn it, the kids are the real reason for living. Without them, I just can't see the purpose.

DB: You're saying then that you believe your children will give your life meaning. You assume that without them there is no direction or purpose to your life.

Tom: Yes, that's it. But they have to be *my* children. I have to produce them. I know it's the wrong thing to say, but without your *own* children, you're just babysitting! I'm not interested in a family of other people's kids. I don't need that at all. I'm not a daycare center. Why should I be interested if the kids aren't mine? [Pause.] Awgh, the whole thing's crazy.

DB: I hear emotion in your voice right now. What are you feeling?

Tom: Nothing! What's the use in calling attention to it? Nothing will change.

DB: It helps to express it.

Tom: Why? The whole situation's a mess. It doesn't get any better. It only gets worse. I really feel terrible about myself. What good is my success at work or my marriage to Barbara if I can't have children? I look around me and even the most miserable of men can do what I can't. I'm a failure. A washout. This is the most important life function and I'm deficient. What matters most eludes me. What matters least I have plenty of. It's not fair. And no one understands. Friends are no help at all. They say the wrong thing despite their good intentions. No, this is something I have to face alone, even without Barbara. I can't talk to her. She feels sorry for me, and she's angry at me. And why shouldn't she be? I can't give her what she wants. The whole thing hurts me in the pit of my stomach. I want to cry, but it's just not right. I shouldn't be so weak. [He cries, at first softly, then deeply, breaking into sobs.] I'm sorry. I lost it. I didn't realize how much feeling I had stored up inside me.

DB: I'm glad you could express it. Your disappointment has created a good deal of anger and sadness.

Tom: Yeah. This is one subject I guess I have deep feelings about. [Pause. He looks out the window, then back at me.] I feel a little clearer now.

DB: I'm glad to hear that. It helps to let out what's been stored up for a long time. [Pause.] I know we've been over this before in a general way, but let me ask you more directly this time: Is your expectation to father children biologically possible?

Tom: I thought for a long time that it was, and I tried all sorts of remedies, but if I'm honest with myself I know it isn't.

DB: So you're disappointed about something that can't be attained no matter what you do.

Tom: I guess that's true. But I can't seem to give it up.

DB: I think you *can*. You're capable of surrendering the expectation. What you really mean is that you still choose not to. You *won't*.

Tom: Okay, I agree. I won't. It's hard to.

DB: I know it's hard. You see your expectation of fatherhood as essential to you. I wonder if it really is?

Tom: Of course it is. It's very important to me.

DB: There's no question that you want very badly to father children and that you seek meaning in your life through fatherhood. But I doubt that either of these wishes are essential to your happiness. You would have preferred them, naturally, but they aren't indispensable. I wonder, in fact, how these expectations have *limited* your experience.

Tom: What are you getting at?

DB: Well, in placing so much emphasis on family and the fathering of your own children, you seem to have excluded other possibilities from your life which would also provide meaning and significance. For example, creative endeavors, spiritual pursuits, and community service can all give you intrinsic satisfaction and purpose. Fatherhood may be important, but surely it's not everything.

Tom: I see what you mean, but I'm still not convinced. Why shouldn't I get what I want? It's not fair that I shouldn't! Everybody's having unwanted pregnancies, and here Barbara and I want a baby so badly.

DB: You give the impression you feel entitled to your expectation. That it's something owed to you simply because you strongly desire it.

Tom: In a way that's how I feel—almost like a kid who sulks when he doesn't get what he wants. My disappointment is like sulking. I know I'm holding onto my hurt. Underneath it all I feel somehow injured because I didn't get what I expected.

DB: What do you suppose is the payoff in being disappointed?

Tom: Payoff? You must be joking. Why would I want to feel disappointed?

DB: It does sound strange, I admit, but it's equally strange that you would hold onto an expectation that's clearly impossible to meet. There must be another reason for doing so—a payoff that we can't easily see.

Tom: Yeah, but I can't imagine what it could be.

DB: What's the effect of your feeling disappointed?

Tom: Well, I'm miserable. That much is clear. And I feel sorry for myself. I feel wronged and victimized, like the world has treated me shabbily.

DB: Is there any payoff in those feelings?

Tom: In a way, yeah. I feel a bit like a romantic but tragic hero. I have to admit I like those feelings once in a while. Here I am walking around the world seemingly in control of my destiny, but I have one tragic flaw, like Hamlet. It's a strange role. I'm fascinated by it, I guess, but I hardly think it explains why I became disappointed.

DB: You're right in the sense that the tragic role may not

have motivated you to be disappointed. But once you were, the role became a convenient and attractive way to tolerate your dilemma. Now it's hard to give it up.

Tom: I see what you mean. That seems to fit. [Pause. He appears to go inward.]

DB: Tom, you look deep in thought. I wonder what sorts of things you're saying to yourself?

Tom: So you think I talk to myself. I'm not that bad off yet!

DB: Everyone talks to themselves. Most people do it privately inside their heads. This kind of talking is called an internal dialogue. We hardly know it's happening. For example, if I fail an exam I might say to myself, "How stupid can I be? I should have studied harder. Now I'm in real trouble." Or I might say, "The test was unfair; the subject was boring. This is no reflection on me." We talk to ourselves as we experience things and in so doing we influence the way we feel. We interpret our experiences and then react to those interpretations. I wonder what you've been saying to yourself.

Tom: Now that you mention it, I was thinking a few things as we talked.

DB: Such as?

Tom: Well, first I thought, "He's just trying to trick me to give up what I want. Since there's no orange juice left, he wants me to be satisfied with apple juice." That sort of thing. But I still want orange juice. Then I thought, "I'm not suited for anything but fatherhood. I'm not creative; I don't have any spiritual leanings. Community service isn't for me. Fatherhood—that's the only thing I can do. If I just had the chance." After this I began to feel again how unfair the situation was. I thought to myself, "It's just not right. I would make such a good father, while others with children go around abusing them or taking them for granted."

DB: All these internal statements show your resistance to accepting your situation and making change. You focus on what you lose rather than what you gain. You downplay your interest and aptitude for other meaningful activity. You continue to convince yourself that fatherhood is indispensable. And you replay the unfairness of it all when you know full well that life is rarely just. These statements can help to forestall change and keep you disappointed. They prevent acceptance of your dilemma and movement out of your frustration.

Tom: My problem keeps getting clearer. Really, I have to accept my situation and give up the impossible expectations... well, not so much give them up but change them to something more realistic.

DB: Do you have anything in mind?

Tom: Well, I've never let myself consider this before, but I can still be a father. Barbara and I could adopt a child or we could use donor sperm. There are other possibilities.

DB: That's true. But they only seem viable once you've accepted the failure of your original expectations.

Tom: I never saw it that way before.

DB: Sometimes for the fog to lift a little wind is necessary.

Tom: Now, what does that mean?

DB: A Chinese proverb. Think about it.

Moving Up from Disappointment

As a result of our talk, Tom was able to accept his disappointment and eventually create more realistic second-order expectations for himself. A look back at our conversation will show the steps I helped him to take. First, he *acknowledged disappointment* as the cause of his confusion and turmoil. Then he *identified* not just the *failed expectation* but also the *deeper wish* contained within it. And as he went through these steps, his *feelings of anger and sadness welled up and he expressed*

them in sharp words followed by tears. With the emotional
edge removed, he *recognized the impossibility* of his expectation, but was not yet ready to relinquish it. At this point, I
asked a series of questions to help him gain a new perspective
on his wishes and to show him how he *resisted change* by making counterproductive *internal statements*. Having gone
through this process, he was in a position to accept his situation
and create a second-order expectation.

To move up from disappointment, we must follow a sequence similar to Tom's.

Step One: Acknowledging Disappointment
Step Two: Feeling and Expressing the Emotions
Step Three: Sorting Out the Issues
Step Four: Reaching Acceptance
Step Five: Moving On

Step One: Acknowledging Disappointment

We would think acknowledging disappointment would be
a relatively simple process—like recognizing an itch or the
desire to eat. Surprisingly, this is not the case. Like Tom,
many of us are so caught up in our misery that we fail to see
the disappointment at its root. Tom knew he was deeply
disappointed, but his anger and self-pity were more obvious:
They dominated his experience and blocked him from facing
his dilemma squarely. It is only by taking the time to ask,
"What is at the root of my feeling?" that we can get a glimpse
of the sometimes obscure nature of disappointment.

Some people prefer to avoid looking directly at their disappointments. Refusal to identify one's difficulties is grounded
in the magical belief that they will go away if we just ignore

them. Like ostriches, we may prefer to bury our heads in the sand and wait until the danger passes. But, of course, such tactics are counterproductive. The fact is that facing disappointment is the initial step in moving out of it.

Remember that every disappointment is a conflict between wish and reality. The tension that exists between these two contending forces will continue as long as the failure of the expectation has not been accepted.

Step Two: Feeling and Expressing the Emotions (Emotional Processing)

The feelings associated with letdown—anger, hurt, self-pity, loss, dispossession—cannot be denied or suppressed without paying a price, usually the persistence of disappointment. Anyone who has ever tried to avoid bereavement knows that such attempts backfire into depression, confusion, and psychosomatic disorders. Likewise, when couples deny their anger toward each other, their feelings usually end up leaking out in the form of nitpicking, complaining, or obstinacy. The value of feeling one's emotions is an accepted assumption in our psychologically sophisticated age. What is forgotten is that the *expression* of such feelings is of equal importance. Such action has two functions. One, it keeps us from becoming emotionally frigid. Like a finely tuned engine, our affective parts require use or they will rust into inaccessibility. And two, it allows feelings to be discharged and thereby completed. The unexpressed emotion lingers longer than the expressed emotion.

Some feelings, however, are hurtful or dangerous. How are these to be expressed without dire consequences? Here are two effective formats—one verbal, one written—which have helped many people who tend to store up their emotions.

Format A: Find a responsible friend who's willing to listen. Seek out a private spot where sound will not be a problem. Set a time limit and ask your companion to watch the clock for you. Ten to fifteen minutes should suffice. Then express your feelings of disappointment as graphically and with as much feeling as you can muster. Discharge your frustration and accompanying emotional pain. Allow yourself to cry if you feel sadness. This is an opportunity to ventilate feeling safely. Allow yourself to reach a crescendo of expression. At the designated time, stop, breathe deeply into your abdomen, and relax. If you don't feel some immediate relief, continue the breathing until you experience a sense of lightness. Measure the change in your mood.

If a friend is not available, use the same procedure, imagining that you are talking to such a person.

Format B: Find a private place, free of disturbance. Bring a pen and paper with you. Meditate for a few minutes about your feelings. Visualize yourself at the moment you first experienced the disappointment. Then write about your experience in the present tense, focusing on your emotional reaction. Do you feel anger, frustration, hurt, loss, self-pity, depression? Don't be critical of what you write and don't rework any of it. This is not a short-story contest. The end product is not nearly as important as the process of doing it. Let your feelings flow from your pen. When you have nothing more to say, sit with yourself for a few minutes and measure the effect of the exercise. If you still feel agitated, write about it. If you are more relaxed, move onto the next step in the sequence.

In our conversation, ventilation of feeling helped Tom to express the backlog of built-up anger and sadness so that he felt receptive enough to analyze his situation and consider change. Most therapists agree that patients are rarely able to solve their problems while they feel overwhelmed by strong emotion. We all know that making change in a relationship, or even an institution, is almost impossible when the participants are angry, fearful, or ecstatic. Once people have vented their feelings and calmed down, clear thinking and rational action are possible. Emotional catharsis is not a solution in itself but a necessary precondition for change. It sets the stage for more mindful intervention.

Step Three: Sorting Out the Issues (Intellectual Processing)

This step has four parts: identifying the expectation, uncovering the lifewish, recognizing the faulty premise, and gaining perspective on the experience.

Identifying the Expectation: Once we have allowed expression of feeling, we must look for the unmet expectation that causes our deepest frustration. Ask yourself, "What am I disappointed about?" "What did I expect to happen?" If nothing obvious is forthcoming, perhaps you don't want to acknowledge the answer. Some expectations are troubling in themselves and can be blocked from awareness with or without conscious intent. For example, the bride who expects her groom to be acceptable to her parents may not wish to recognize the expectation. She may fear such desires will alienate her new husband, who thinks he has only to please her. Or the lover who expects every sexual experience to be an earthquake with fireworks may know deep in her bones that such a situation represents an impossible wish. But she refuses to acknowledge her expectation in an effort to keep her sexual fantasy intact.

Of course, not all expectations are difficult to recognize. Some are like Tom's desire to father his own children—clear and inescapable. These expectations are as sirens wailing in the night; we can't help but hear them screaming for attention.

Uncovering the Lifewish: Recognizing the expectation on the other side of disappointment is a relatively simple task when compared with exposing the deeper wish. I have noted that every expectation contains within it a simple wish for an outcome and a deeper wish about the nature of life. These wishes are artifacts from an earlier time when we held a naive view of the world. It is the deeper lifewish within every expectation that hooks us and maintains our emotional investment. Awareness of these wishes is sometimes enough to motivate us to let go of them, but generally we need additional coaxing before we are ready to give them up.

In identifying the wish component within the expectation, we find that a single thought may contain many levels of desire. For example, "I expect my spouse and my parents to get along well" indicates a wish for one's life partner and parents to establish and maintain their own relationship. But it also implies a yearning for the significant persons in one's life to like each other. At the deepest level, the owner of this expectation may be hoping for a world in which human relations exist without conflict. If you have difficulty uncovering your deepest wishes, you might tease them out using the rhetorical question provoked by every loss—"Why can't circumstances be different?" Reflect on your disappointed expectation and then ask, "Why can't this world be..." completing the sentence with the implied wish of the expectation. For example, the failure of friends to unconditionally support your actions produces the question, "Why can't the world be more accepting and less critical?" The deeper wish is for life to be free of undermining experiences and filled with validating interactions. The failure of your first book to make it to the bestseller list elicits, "Why can't the world give me what I want?" The underlying wish is for life to gratify your desires. In Tom's case, two wishes are apparent: the desire for parenthood which will endow life with meaning and purpose, and the wish to maintain the family lineage, which suggests a more profound hope for immortality through the fathering of future generations.

. These lifewishes have an illusionary character. We can never find immortality, unqualified love, or conflict-free human relations. But we want these things nonetheless. Hard as it is to acknowledge, we still wish for fairy tales to come true.

Below is a list of common lifewishes. Use it to help you identify the deeper wish contained in your expectations.

The wish for life to be easy
The wish for everything to remain the same
The wish for love alone to suffice
The wish for life to be fair
The wish for life to be exciting

The wish for security
The wish to be saved
The wish to be taken care of
The wish to be special
The wish to be perfect
The wish for life to be conflict-free
The wish to be loved
The wish to live forever
The wish for things to be as we want them

Recognizing the Faulty Premise: The problem is not in maintaining wishes but in believing in their possibility. If we did not take them seriously, did not convert them into operational premises that influence attitude and action, we would not be disappointed by their failure. But these unrealistic yearnings have a way of gaining the upper hand. They easily overrun the slim boundary between what we want and what we expect. For example, the wish for life to be easy, so prominent in the midlife years, is transformed into the illusional belief that life *should*, *can*, or *will* be easy. Likewise, the desire to be perfect becomes "I *can* exist without fault." At the root of every disappointment, then, is a lifewish that has been changed into a working but faulty expectation that fails and causes letdown.

Tom's lifewish to gain some measure of immortality through his children is common enough. Yet it is a highly unrealistic hope, subject to the deterioration and distortion of each succeeding generation's memory. Tom didn't see his lifewish as just another fantasy. On the contrary, he thought of it as real possibility. It is one thing to dream, another to expect those dreams to be realized. This is the faulty premise that needs to be recognized.

254 IS THAT ALL THERE IS?

Gaining Perspective: When we are in the throes of disappointment, it is hard to sort out the meaning of the experience. We tend to exaggerate its importance and endow our disappointments with symbolic implications. A filmmaker patient of mine whose work was inadvertently left out of a press screening feared that his situation was a replay of a hardluck childhood pattern. The thought that he might be falling back into an old and detested "life script" made it hard for him to see his circumstances clearly. Sometimes we interpret circumstances correctly; other times we construe the surrender of a failed expectation as a sign that our world view is about to collapse and take us with it. We hold onto disappointment as a way to save our illusions about life.

It is important in sorting out each situation to gain perspective on our disappointment. This action can be accomplished by taking the following measures:

1. *Viewing each disappointment as a singular event without attaching it to past or future implications.* (Such implications need investigation at another time, but they only get in the way here.) From this unencumbered standpoint, we can accept our present condition without excessive fear or anxiety. The symbolic meaning has been extricated. The experience is just as it appears: We expected an outcome which did not occur. The issue is straightforward and uncluttered by portents.

2. *Understanding that our expectations are not indispensable to our future happiness.* Of course we prefer that they succeed, but desire and necessity should not be confused. We require food to survive but not a Rolls Royce to transport it home. Tom initially confused the two, but eventually saw

that his life could have meaning without his expectation of fatherhood being realized.

3. *Recognizing that we are not guaranteed or entitled to our expectations.* Just because we expect a good sexual relationship or a high-paying job does not mean we are owed either. To believe we have a right to every wish is to distort our relationship to satisfaction. It is well to remember that we are guaranteed the pursuit of happiness, but not the happiness itself.

Below are three short-order exercises that can also be used to gain a new perspective on the failed expectation.

Observing the Disappointed Self: Find a comfortable, quiet place and relax for ten minutes, breathing fully and regularly into your abdomen and chest. Now close your eyes and get an image of a ball rolling down a hill. Follow it with your mind's eye. Repeat the sequence several times. Get an image of a pen slowly drawing a circle. Follow the motion. Repeat several times.

Consider this thought. Each of us is a composite of many minor selves which taken together compose our personality. There is the hurt child, the pining romantic, the rebellious hero, the free spirit, and so forth. Become aware of the disappointed part of yourself, the defeated, crestfallen side of you. Allow an image of this part to emerge. Don't push to create the image or judge what you see. Just observe it as if you were watching television. What is its shape and color? What are the feelings that emanate from it? Allow it to speak to you and listen carefully to its words. Let the image fade away into the background. Be aware of what you now feel.

This exercise, loosely based on the psychosynthesis techniques of Roberto Assagioli, helps to distinguish the essential self from its minor parts. By observing your disappointment you separate from it, since the act of looking requires that you be removed from what you're looking at. Once separated, the subself loses much of its power to overwhelm and a new relationship to disappointment is created.

Memory Lane: Find a comfortable, quiet place and relax for ten minutes, breathing fully and regularly into your abdomen and chest. On a piece of paper, write down five past disappointments, each occurring at least one year ago. Write in detail how you felt while these experiences were happening. Consider how you feel about these disappointments today. What does this comparison tell you?

In examining past letdowns, you become aware of the temporal nature of disappointment and recognize your ability to move beyond a particular loss.

Advising Yourself: Find a comfortable, quiet place and relax for ten minutes, breathing freely and regularly into your abdomen and chest. Identify your disappointment and the failed expectation underlying it. In your mind, create a detailed scenario in which a similar disappointment is experienced by a friend. How does the person react? What feelings does he/she express? Now imagine that he/she approaches you for advice on how to deal with the situation. What would you say? How would you say it so that it could be heard with a receptive ear? Now apply the advice to yourself. What effect does it have?

By separating from the personal experience and observing it in the life of another person, you gain a more objective frame of reference. This distance allows the full use of your problem-solving abilities which may have been blocked by strong feelings of loss.

Step Four: Reaching Acceptance

Having moved through emotional and intellectual processing, we are now in a better position to accept our disappointments—to move them from the foreground of our attention to the background where they can simply fade away. The final stage in the disappointment process involves acceptance of the lost expectation. This does not mean we are necessarily happy with the circumstances or that we tacitly approve of them. It simply means that we accept rather than deny what exists. It is only by accepting our disappointments that we can prevent them from happening again.

Yet, in spite of the fact that it makes no apparent sense to continue playing a losing hand, many people remain unwilling to lay down their failed expectations and get up from the table. Human beings may have the capacity to behave rationally but they don't always use it. They frequently make choices that sabotage their longer-range interests and goals. Tom, for example, had to come to grips with his resistance to acknowledging his loss before he could develop a second-order expectation.

Below are two common obstacles to fully accepting the reality of our failed expectations:

Self-Talk: We resist resolving disappointment by actually programming ourselves with negative self-talk. The noted psychiatrist Eric Berne used the term "internal dialogue" to describe the way in which we speak to ourselves as we experience daily events. For example, when we get angry at an insulting remark, our response is usually preceded by a statement to ourselves like, "That so and so. Who is he to treat me like that?" Or, in a more positive vein, when we fall down on the ski slope we might say, "It doesn't matter. The fall is of no consequence," and continue down the mountain. Our attitude toward an event is largely constructed on such preconscious statements to the self. These thoughts are not always immediately accessible, but they can be inferred or observed if we pay careful attention to our thinking. Thus we have the power to influence our attitudes toward occurrences by inhibiting certain statements or encouraging others.

Tom observed that he had been conducting an internal dialogue during our conversation. The comments he made to himself prevented him from sorting out his situation. Here are several types of internal statements used to delay or suppress change.

1. *Catastrophic Statements:* These will generally read: "If this occurs, then something terrible will happen." Examples: "If my friend doesn't love me, I will die unloved and uncared for!" or "If the world isn't fair, what's the sense of living?" or "If I surrender my expectation to be special, I will be nothing!"

Speaking to oneself in this manner creates panic and fear. Relinquishing an expectation or wish becomes associated with catastrophe. Since the consequences are so exaggerated, the individual sees only one sensible choice: to prevent the debacle from occurring by maintaining the status quo.

2. *Hopeless Statements*: These internal considerations reflect the passive attitude that even if changes were possible, they

would not do any good. Examples: "What's the use of speaking to my husband about my disappointment? Nothing will change!" or "Even if I were friendlier or worked harder, my boss still wouldn't like me," or "My children and I are not on the same wavelength. Talking to them is pointless."

Hopeless statements drain motivation for change and negate any desire to take remedial action. One can suffer a massive case of alienation by continually programming resignation into the mind's data bank.

3. *Fatalistic Statements*: This pattern is a variation on the above. The dialogue rests on the premise that individuals have no control over their lives. Common statements to the self include: "Disappointment is my fate—what can I do?" or "Someone up there doesn't like me!" or "It's just my bad luck to have such a disappointing family."

By programming the self to feel that there is no control over destiny, deterministic statements encourage acceptance of the most unsatisfying conditions and undermine attempts at change.

The Big Payoff: When there is a hidden payoff in remaining disappointed, we may resist resolution. The trouble with most of these "secondary gains" is that they are not worth the price of continued disillusionment and resignation. Take, for example, the individual, disappointed by her friends, who holds onto her feelings in order to support a neurotic view of herself as undesirable. Or perhaps she is really playing the role of martyr—someone who has been wronged and enjoys the sense of righteousness that unjust treatment allows. Tom's payoff was less extreme. Despite his complaints, the role of a successful but tragically flawed man held attraction for him. In the end, however, his romantic misfortune was unsatisfying, and he chose to relinquish it.

Payoffs come in many shapes and sizes. When we hold

onto dashed expectations, we support feelings that are not in our long-range or true interests. Remaining disappointed comes not just from a resistance to accepting the failed outcome but also from the neurotic profit gained by feeling miserable. Individuals who have a need to suffer or wish others to feel sorry for them will be drawn to the odd advantages of getting stuck in disappointment.

Step Five: Moving On: Rachel's Story

Paradoxically, accepting disappointment is the step that allows us to move on to the creation of second-order expectations. To understand how surrendering failed expectation can help us to gain what we want, let us consider the situation of Rachel, a talented, twenty-seven-year-old actress, who, until she began dating Bob, had never been in a successful long-term relationship. Although they seemed compatible, Bob, who had been divorced just six months before, was hesitant to make a commitment of any sort. He expressed this sentiment almost from the outset. Rachel accepted the situation but did not really appreciate the depth of his feelings. She continued to hope that with time he would warm to the idea of a deeper involvement. She assumed the divorce had left temporary wounds that eventually would heal.

Rachel and Bob usually spent two evenings a week together and frequently called each other on off-days. They shared an interest in the performing arts, often went to museums and galleries, and spent long hours discussing politics. They agreed on almost everything but the current state of their relationship, a subject they seemed to avoid by unspoken mutual consent. When Bob suggested they travel together across the country on a shared vacation, Rachel jumped at the chance. She saw it as a real opportunity to deepen their ties and cement their commitment to each other. With enthusiasm, she set about planning every detail of the trip. She investigated the most scenic routes. She made motel reservations in advance. She planned amusing day-excursions. Excited by the odyssey, she looked forward to the trip with great anticipation. "So much sustained time with Bob," she thought, "will be wonderfully romantic. No stress from work, no responsibilities—a really carefree holiday."

As the time approached, Bob seemed more distant. He blamed his inaccessibility on the pressures of finishing a specific project before their vacation. Rachel was somewhat alarmed but accepted the explanation. After all, this was not the first time that he had been very busy. When they finally drove over the bridge and out of town, she assumed he would relax and reconnect with her. Indeed, the deepening of their intimacy was her primary expectation for the vacation. Rachel was hoping for more than just a good time; she wanted the trip to bring about a change in their relationship.

But it didn't happen that way. Although they sat only two feet apart in her car, Bob seemed cooler and more distant than she could ever remember. At the Grand Canyon, she attempted to confront his inaccessibility, but he changed the subject and she gave up without trying again. A pattern emerged. They were both cheerful in the morning, but fatigued and mildly depressed by afternoon. They carried on conversations about the usual subjects, the natural wonders they were seeing and the strange sea of tourists around them, but the moment Rachel broached the issue of their relationship, Bob withdrew and became moody. After a while, she simply resigned herself to superficial conversation. When they returned home, she withdrew to her apartment, took a long walk, and found herself crying.

Rachel recognized her disappointment and the expectation that had gone unmet. In spite of her awareness of Bob's ambivalence toward their relationship, she had hoped he would come around as they spent more time together. As things turned out, it was an unrealistic hope, based on a lifewish for circumstances to be as she wanted them, not as they in fact were. But Rachel refused to be daunted by her disappointment. She had cried and felt the pain of her experience, but having allowed her emotions free expression, she determined not to stay caught up in her misery.

She evaluated her situation and saw that although her expectations for the trip had failed, her desire for a more committed relationship was still attainable if she took different action. Of course, if she simply went on as usual, nothing would change. For all she knew, Bob might behave in the same manner indefinitely. No, if she really wanted a deeper commitment, she would have to deal differently with the situation.

Rachel weighed the price of pursuing a more serious relationship with Bob and decided it was worth the risk in possible rejection and greater disappointment. Her plan was to talk to him about the vacation in a relaxed environment where she could express her feelings openly. She called him and arranged for a long dinner at her place. All afternoon she was anxious, but after he arrived and they exchanged pleasantries, she gathered up her courage and told him about her feelings. Bob responded to her candor with forthrightness; he was feeling guilty and needed to clear his own conscience. He confessed that although he had wanted to vacation with her, as the time approached he became more and more nervous. He thought the long hours together in the car would trap him. He imagined that eventually, out of exhaustion, he would let down his defenses and get closer to her than was comfortable. As a result, he kept his distance by withdrawing emotionally from the situation. He knew she was upset by his actions, but he feared the possibility of unwanted commitment even more.

As they talked openly, both recognized that a genuine affection existed between them. Speaking honestly and from the heart had cleared the air. Rachel understood for the first time Bob's fears and anxieties about repeating a past hurt. Bob realized that if he showed his vulnerability, Rachel would not overwhelm or manipulate the situation for her own gain. The interaction showed them both that they could trust each other. The talk placed the relationship on a new level, and the emotional bond between the two was strengthened without Rachel pushing or Bob feeling threatened. A positive experience was born out of disappointment.

By taking this course of action, Rachel had inadvertently written a second-order expectation. She no longer expected the commitment would just happen as a result of long hours spent together. She now recognized that unless she took the risk of talking to Bob, few changes were likely. Her new expectation was more realistic, and the results were happily favorable.

Had Rachel wallowed in her initial disappointment, she

would have become so embittered or passive that change would have been unthinkable. Instead, she kept her eye on her long-range interests and adapted to the demands of the situation.

Looking Back

Because disappointment is a particular form of loss, moving through it—from the failure of expectation to the final acceptance—follows a specific pattern. Once disappointed, there are four steps we can take to speed that process. These are: acknowledging the disappointment, feeling and expressing the emotions, sorting out the issues, and reaching acceptance. It is only after we accept the loss of our wishes that we are free enough to create new, educated expectations in order to prevent recurrences of disappointment.

For people like Tom, who refuse to relinquish their expectations even while recognizing their impossibility, the extrication process is of special benefit. Using it, they can ventilate the feelings associated with loss (anger, frustration, hurt, self-pity, panic) and "reframe" their expectations in a new light so that they can be relinquished. Ultimately, accepting disappointment requires surrendering the belief that one's lifewishes require satisfaction. Giving up these illusional wishes is in our long-range interest because they prevent us from accepting not only our immediate disappointment but the nature of life as well.

Making Disappointment Work for You

*Failure is, in a sense, the highway to success, inasmuch as
every discovery of what is false leads us to seek earnestly
after what is true, and every fresh experience points out some
form of error which we shall afterward carefully avoid.*
                                                        John Keats

Most people view disappointment as a negative, unredeemable experience without value or merit. Like mildew, a sprained ankle, or a broken seat at the movie theater, they consider it a regrettable condition to be avoided whenever possible. In chronic form, disappointment is more than regrettable. It is a bridge that links resignation with despair, a causeway to melancholia and depression. Yet, in its milder versions, disappointment *does* have a positive side. More than that, it is quite functional and plays a very important role in all human endeavor. Disappointment can actually be an ally in the search for contentment and personal happiness. Provided we use it to our advantage and don't allow it to take on chronic proportions, it has value as a teacher and motivator. Disappointment can work for you. Those who

265

have learned from it in the past have less of it in their future. They seem to move through it more rapidly.

The Value of Negative Experience

Most experience, whether positive or negative, has something to teach us. Bad experiences usually convey a more urgent message because they are threatening, frustrating, or anxiety-provoking. As the behavioral psychologists are fond of pointing out, how we respond in the present is determined to a large extent by the learning (or conditioning) in our past. Suppose you burn your tongue while eating a steaming bowl of soup. Next time you'll probably wait until the soup cools or, if you're impatient, blow on the contents of the next spoonful. Negative experience has warned you of the consequences of a particular action. It has provided a lesson about soup and perhaps about impatience. Because of your burnt tongue, you are a wiser, albeit more cautious, diner. Bad experience also shakes you out of lethargy. Human beings tend to be creatures of habit. We move through life in a walking sleep, repeating the same actions week in and out, and even using the same groups of muscles to do so. Our capacity for repetition is enormous. Most of us repeat, without major variation, a daily sequence from the sound of the alarm clock to the moment of sleep sixteen hours later. Our existence is ritualized in this manner to avoid discomfort and anxiety, but often we risk becoming mechanized, complacent, and dull, trading excitement for security. A negative experience is like a slap in the face or a drenching in ice water. It wakes us up to our surroundings again, calls forth our energy, and challenges us to new action.

The benefits of this reawakening sometimes outweigh the consequences of the bad experience.

In the process of reacting we must reassess our situation. This evaluation can produce healthy change. We stop taking our lives for granted and begin to act with intention and awareness. For example, when someone we love dies, we feel prolonged, deep grief. But the process of loss provides some benefit as well. It readjusts our priorities and clarifies what is important. Trivial concerns and worries fade away. They seem inconsequential by comparison with the loss of life. Death offers survivors a message about how to proceed with the business of living. It tells them that life is too short and precarious to spend on useless and mundane struggles.

Similarly, frustration—another negative condition we try to avoid—is invaluable in aiding psychological growth, especially during infancy and early childhood. Psychiatrist Margaret Mahler has even suggested that frustration, balanced with a positive relationship to the mother, helps to develop the child's autonomy and ego strength. It fosters the infant's maturity by nudging her on to new action independent of the help of her primary parent. Such a level of frustration must be strong enough to develop conflict-solving capacities by forcing the child to seek her own solutions, and weak enough to allow the new baby some gratification and comfort. In adulthood, the situation is basically similar. Some frustration sharpens our intellect and discourages indolence. Too much is overwhelming and undermines us.

Disappointment, as one more negative experience, shakes us up and provokes reassessment of our circumstances. But it does much more than this. It functions in our behalf by teaching us about the limits of possibility, motivating us to take positive action, and maybe even strengthening our resolve. Let us investigate how this bogeyman can be used to our advantage.

Disappointment: Our First Teacher

How do we learn about the limits of reality? Psychologists differ considerably on this issue, but folk knowledge is quite clear. Life itself teaches us, with a bit of help from teachers and formal education. Consider how this process occurs. During the first months of life, the infant's bodily sensations are all that is real to it. Hunger, pain, fatigue, delight are the infant's entire universe. Even the primary parent is experienced as part of self. Slowly and inconsistently, the infant begins to distinguish objects. As this gradual process takes place, the baby's developing sense of reality outside itself is actually encouraged by disappointment. In fact, Freud, in his paper "Formulations in the Two Principles of Mental Functioning" (1911), writes that it is disappointment over not getting expected satisfaction that leads the child to supplement fantasy with objective evaluation and judgment of the external world—the "reality principle." Put simply, early disappointment motivates the infant to investigate and evaluate the world. By using memory, perception, and thought, it learns to distinguish what is real from what is imagined. Over time, the child becomes proficient at sizing up reality.

Disappointment also educates us about the reality of possibility. It is through the process of losing an expectation that we learn what is possible. As a young boy, I once sent in a cereal boxtop to get a genuine Canadian Mountie badge. The next day I went to the mailbox to search for my gift. It

wasn't there. I was stricken with disappointment. I complained for hours. It ruined my day and, needless to say,
my mother's. By the time the badge arrived six weeks later,
I had learned a powerful and important lesson. Expectations
of immediate gratification are not always met. Sometimes
we simply have to wait. Not only did I develop an understanding of delayed reward (and incidentally, the vagaries of
postal service), but I also began to see that merely expecting
(wishing) did not produce a result.

We might think of disappointment as a "possibility meter."
Each loss of expectation gives us a reading on how well we
have assessed possibility. If an expectation fails, it tells us
something about its attainability. Paying attention to this
feedback, we can learn to avoid disappointment in the future
by shaping our expectations differently—developing what I
have called second-order expectations. We may find out that
X is attainable and Y is possible only under certain circumstances, or we may realize that none of our expectations is
realistic. We need only read the meter. A friend of mine,
Sarah, used an experience of disappointment to create new,
more realistic expectations. Her male intimate of two months
failed to show up for an exhibition of her paintings. This was
an important event in her life, and she was disappointed and
resentful. She accepted his inadequate excuse, though she
trusted him less because it seemed like a false alibi. At
another showing of her work three months later, he was
again conspicuously missing. Sarah was let down once more,
but this time she opened her eyes to the lesson contained
in her disappointment. She recognized that her expectations
for an intimate and sharing relationship with this man were
probably unrealistic. She wanted a partner who would be
more interested in her life and take her involvement in art

seriously. She was faced with a choice: change the expectation or exchange the man. Her disappointment meter had told her twice that he was not reliable or interested in an important part of her identity.

Disappointment is the sort of condition we would prefer to avoid. Yet experiencing it gives us the opportunity to fine-tune our view of possibility. Ironically, those who learn from dashed expectations are those who avoid chronic disappointment. The best teacher of how to avoid disappointment is disappointment itself.

Consider the educational value of disappointment in another way—as a cold shower that dampens our illusions and wishes. Our childhood hopes are carried around like old baggage on life's journey, and we are hard-pressed to give them up. They color every expectation. We have already encountered many of them: the wish for life to be fair, people to remain the same, love alone to sustain us. Disappointment teaches us that these wishes have no basis in reality and that we need to surrender our view that their fulfillment is, in fact, possible.

By putting the damper on our expectations, disappointment forces us to reevaluate our wants. This process encourages maturity. Illusions hold us back from embracing life as it is. The thirty-two-year-old man who is disappointed in how quickly he is aging looks in the mirror each morning and sees wrinkles on his forehead and crow's feet around his eyes. Why is he disappointed? He had expected to appear youthful through middle age. At the root of the expectation is a wish for prolonged youth—to hold back the hands of time. The quest for immortality, the most vain of all human desires, plagues our youth-oriented culture. Even the cover girl—the ideal standard of female beauty—is often too young to vote. Youth is equated with desirability and value. No wonder the man wishes to remain young. The experience of observable aging disturbs him. His deeper wish cannot be satisfied. Only if he is receptive to the lesson contained in his disappointment will he realize that the deeply etched lines on his face will not disappear. His expectation of prolonged youth—eternal youth—is illusory and must be relinquished to avoid greater frustration. His disappointment has provided him with an invitation to reevaluate his unrealistic expectations.

The central illusion at the root of all disappointment is the belief that as individuals we have the right to have all our needs and desires fulfilled. Failed expectation is a form of *un*gratification, a narcissistic injury. We do not get what we think we deserve. Yet, in reality, we cannot always have what we want. Sometimes we must wait for satisfaction. Other times even waiting will not produce the desired result. All disappointment defies the illusional wish that we are entitled to a particular outcome. Disappointment says to us that we are not special but human like everyone else and subject to the laws of nature. There are limits to gratification. Perhaps this is disappointment's most important lesson.

There is yet another way in which disappointment can be useful, a way which offers an independent study course in self. By analyzing your disappointments you learn a great deal about your own character. Chronic patterns of disappointment are as revealing as responses to a Rorschach ink blot. They tell us what we expect from life and from ourselves. For example, repeated disappointment in not receiving enough recognition indicates an underlying wish to be special or a deep need to gain the constant approval of others. Recurrent disappointment in oneself suggests a lack of confidence and a self-critical nature. The clues are easily observed. Try this exercise yourself.

Independent Study: Learning about Yourself from Disappointment.

1. Write down three significant disappointments in your life.

2. Identify the unmet expectations.

3. Identify the deeper wish at the root of each expectation.

4. Ask yourself: A. What sort of patterns exist in these expectations, if any? B. What do these expectations reveal about me?

5. Rate your expectations on the Attainability Continuum. Are they fully attainable, somewhat attainable, partially attainable, or unattainable?

6. Ask yourself: A. Is there a pattern in the degree of attainability? B. If so, what does it indicate about your grasp of realistic possibility? C. What else does the pattern suggest about you?

7. Now ask: A. What action would bring the "somewhat" and "partially" attainable expectations to fruition? B. Since you did not take such action (or you wouldn't be disappointed), what does this reveal about you?

Notice that learning about ourselves from disappointment proceeds along three lines:

1. The pattern of desire in our expectations.

2. The degree of realism in our expectations (can they be gratified?).

3. The degree of passivity that we show in not acting to satisfy our desires.

The pattern of our disappointment provides us with important information about ourselves. The problem is we don't always pay attention. We resent our disappointments, complain about them, and let them control us. We don't see them as useful tools to help us avoid future pain, so we fail to learn from them. We simply try to forget our discomfort as rapidly as possible. We might paraphrase the popular words of George Santayana to read, "Those who cannot learn from disappointment are condemned to repeat it."

Light My Fire: Disappointment as Motivator

Although many people seem to stew in disappointment's unsavory juices, still others are inspired by their discomfort to take action. Something within us—perhaps our spirit—has fallen. We must rise up again. Such a situation can galvanize us to act. Feminist Lucy Stone suggests how disappointment works as a motivating force:

> From the first years to which my memory stretches, I have been a disappointed woman. When, with my brothers, I reached forth after sources of knowledge, I was reproved with "It isn't fit for you; it doesn't belong to women." ... In education, in marriage, in religion, in everything, disappointment is the lot of women. It shall be the business of my life to deepen this disappointment in every woman's heart until she bows down to it no longer.

Stone's assumption is that a deepening of the experience will provoke reaction. Enough disappointment will create the necessary frustration, anger, and pain to make us sit up and take notice of the need for change. This sort of thinking is paradoxical because we actually prescribe more of the problem to produce a solution. Such strategy forms the basis of homeopathic medicine and certain intervention techniques in psychotherapy. From this point of view, the simple cure for chronic disappointment is *more* disappointment. The addition of greater emotional pain makes the situation so intolerable that a previously eschewed change in expectation or action is now sought. Paradoxical interventions work effectively in circumstances characterized by resistance to change or the failure of other remedies to provide benefit. Given the choice, however, most people would avoid an increase in their level of discomfort even to achieve the longer-range goal of diminished disappointment.

Emotional pain does not always have to reach such extreme levels for people to react. Often we see the enlightened individual who is motivated by disappointment to take the necessary steps to satisfy a failed expectation. For example, the pole vaulter, disappointed with his performance at the track meet, goes back to the practice field and works out even harder. Or the lover, disappointed by a recent sexual encounter, sits down with his partner to discuss ways of improving their lovemaking. We might even conclude that disappointment has the capacity to improve problem-solving skills. There is the classic example, known to every psychology student, of the frustrated monkey who sits in his cage while a banana hangs temptingly outside his reach. Try as he may, he can't quite get at it by sticking his arm through the bars. After many trials and disappointments, he notices a stick in the cage. He grabs it, extends it toward the banana, and manipulates it into range. No one has taught him this behavior. Hunger and disappointment combine to motivate the problem-solving sequence. The monkey acts to satisfy his expectation and his appetite. Human beings with greater powers of reasoning are better equipped to attain gratification than their primate cousins. As long as one's expectation is somewhat attainable, the number of problem-solving strategies is endless.

Enhancing Functioning

Adversity strengthens us! Is this old folk wisdom merely rationalization to help us deal with suffering, or is there psychological truth in it? The answer is qualified. Disappointment *may* strengthen us. However, a great deal depends on when and how much we are disappointed. During periods of stress and personal vulnerability, added disappointment can overwhelm us. It may take months just to get out from under it. If the person has limited ego resources—low self-esteem or feelings of inadequacy—disappointment is unlikely to fortify him. It will keep him defeated and resigned. Chronic disappointment patterns have much the same effect. They weaken resolve and result in despair. But the single disappointment, experienced by a relatively healthy individual who moves through it, does work to enhance functioning in two ways: It helps him learn how to deal with loss, and it shows him firsthand that he can survive adversity.

As I noted earlier, disappointment involves loss, but not the severe loss of an object, friend, or life. Disappointment is the loss of an idea, an expectation. Without disastrous consequences, it provides the psychological experience of mild bereavement. Disappointment is a safe practice field where we learn to deal with emotional pain without playing for high stakes. It is a valuable rehearsal for managing more significant loss.

Our reaction to adversity functions as a mirror. Within it, we can see our frailty and strength. Those who rise to overcome obstacles are rewarded with a reflection of their own mastery and perseverance. Like athletes who have run their first marathon, they have learned they have what it takes to make it. In the words of Wendell Phillips, "What is defeat? Nothing but education; nothing but the first step to something better." If we take this attitude, we will be strengthened by our struggle.

Another Paradoxical Perspective

Until recently, the Western world has shown little interest in Oriental thought or religion. But as the planet becomes smaller and our connection with Asia is strengthened by economic and political bridges, the wisdom of the East has begun to seep into our culture. Nowhere is the experience of disappointment seen as positively as through the eyes of the Buddha.

Buddhism offers a unique perspective on disappointment which is helpful simply by its unusual nature. According to its teachings, life is filled with suffering. Sorrow, grief, dissatisfaction, decay, disappointment—these are all described in one word—*duhka*. The cause of this pain rests in the way we live our lives. Because we feel something is lacking or incomplete, we are always trying to set it right. We busy ourselves striving to improve our existence, getting more pleasure, and holding on to it to fill this void. We attempt to wipe out *duhka* by grasping for more and clinging to what we already have. The frenetic desire for pleasure indicated by our emphasis on leisure-time activity and sexuality, the insatiable quest for new adult toys and games, the constant effort toward improving the quality of our lives by expansion and acquisition, these are all signs of grasping for gratification. From the Buddhist point of view, this is an empty struggle. The things that we desire offer us no real satisfaction. They are simply diversions of tinsel and neon devoid of any inherent value. We are continually disappointed because acquiring the new car or the spacious duplex does not in the long run make us feel better about life. The immediate stimulation they provide wears off quickly and we again look for new gratification. Like the heroin addict, we are on a nerve-racking elevator ride: up, down, up, down; excitement followed by emptiness. The real problem is our ambition to improve ourselves.

How do we exit from this captivating elevator? Strangely enough, the answer rests in disappointment itself. Buddhism asserts that the only way we will ever elect to give up our endless pattern of purposeless striving is by being utterly disappointed. In this paradoxical approach, only prolonged emotional pain has the power to show us the error of our ways. When we are truly disappointed, drenched in our own frustration, we will then have the motivation to give up our counterproductive lifestyle and move to a more spiritual path. Chogyam Trungpa, a revered Tibetan Buddhist who has founded numerous communities in this country, says:

> We must surrender our hopes and expectations as well as our fears, and march directly into disappointment, work with disappointment, go into it and make it our way of life, which is a very hard thing to do. Disappointment is a good sign of basic intelligence. It cannot be compared to anything else: it is so

278 IS THAT ALL THERE IS?

sharp, precise, obvious and direct. If we can open, then we suddenly begin to see that our expectations are irrelevant compared with the reality of the situation we are facing.

Disappointment exhausts us. It wears us down so that finally we relinquish our striving expectations and simply live life without anticipation or plan. We accept life as it is, minute by minute, and give up trying to control it through anticipation or wishes. When we stop clutching at clouds we put an end to our own frustration.

Of course, there is a deeper level to this road to liberation. In the Buddhist way of thinking, striving to maintain control over our future and seeking continual gratification are secondary issues. The sense of self that we are trying to please is actually a transitory and discontinuous event which we take to be real and solid like an "illusory circle of fire made by a whirling torch." For Buddhists, the ego does not exist. Disappointment ultimately teaches us this fact by frustrating our attempts to gratify ourselves.

Whether we accept this notion of the impermanent and unknowable self or whether we reject it, Buddhism's message about disappointment provokes us to new ways of thinking about why we are disappointed. Perhaps the continual struggle for more and better gratification is at the root of the problem. As long as we believe the way to personal happiness is through the satiation of every want, we will be trapped in an illusory quest for an impossible satisfaction. Like the phoenix rising from its own ashes, our appetites resurrect themselves after only the briefest of moments. By calling our attention to the self-defeating nature of striving, the Buddhist perspective has value.

Disappointment as Benefactor

Disappointment, the main cause of much frustration and unhappiness, is also a benefactor. It helps us to develop a clearer understanding of the limits of possibility. It shakes us out of our complacency and challenges us to bring our expectations to fruition or surrender them and proceed to other satisfactions. It enhances our functioning by teaching us to deal with loss and providing confidence to survive future adversity.

The experience of disappointment in small doses is a positive sign. It implies that we have enough trust in the future to expect and to hope. A life without any disappointment means that the person has already given up on tomorrow. Nothing is as bleak as the loss of possibility.

It is what we make of our disappointments that determines our future. If we hide from them, we learn nothing. In a sense, we must embrace our disappointments in order to fathom their meaning. With careful observation, we can discover important things about ourselves and the nature of life that will enrich our existence. The individual with fewest disappointments is the one who has learned from past experience. The road away from disappointment involves the creative use of the problem itself.

In a larger sense, disappointment shakes us out of our narcissistic preoccupation with self. It reminds us that gratification of our wishes is not guaranteed and that we are, after all, only human and subject to the vicissitudes of time and chance. In this era of self-exaltation, that is a fair message to take to heart.

Notes

103–104   In the case: *Ibid.*, p. 25.
105   "I feel like I'm": *Ibid.*, p. 20.
106   "I feel I was": *Ibid.*, p. 24.
107   "I met a traveller": Percy Bysshe Shelley, *The Selected Poetry and Prose*, Modern Library Edition (New York: Random House, 1951).
114   "The motion picture": Marshall McLuhan, *The Medium Is the Message* (New York: Bantam, 1967), p. 131.
114   "When the movies": Marshall McLuhan, *Understanding Media* (New York: McGraw Hill, 1964), p. 231.

PAGE **Chapter 6**

125–26   These four arenas: Daniel Yankelovich, *New Rules* (New York: Random House, 1981), p. 104, 89, 94.
127–28   Impermanent and highly: Divorce Statistics from U.S. Bureau of the Census, "Current Population Reports," Series P-20, #349, and U.S. National Center for Health Statistics.
128   And the median: U.S. National Center for Health Statistics, "Vital Statistics of the United States." Annual and unpublished data, 1978.
128   "Single person households": Yankelovich, *op. cit.*, pp. xiv, 98.
128   With these shifts: *Ibid.*, pp. 97–99.
145   A comparison of Gallup polls: *Psychology Today*, Newsline, April 1982.
170   Absenteeism: *U.S. News and World Report*, April 1981, pp. 71–72.
146   In a recent poll: *Saturday Review*, May 1980.
147   In fact, a University: Yankelovich, *op. cit.*, p. 44.
148   "Maybe some people": *Society*, January/February 1981.
154   In a 1979 survey: Yankelovich, *op. cit.*, p. 96, 98.

PAGE **Chapter 10**

204   "And what wine": Soren Kierkegaard, *Either/Or*, Volume 1.
206   "We love to expect": Samuel Johnson, *Quotations Treasury*.
211   "Life is not": Sam Keen, *What to Do When You're Bored and Blue* (Wyden Books, 1980), p. 152.

PAGE **Chapter 11**

231   In a 1978: *Better Homes and Gardens*, "What's Happening to

the American Family? A Report from More than 300,000 Readers," June 1978, Vol. 56.

232   "A person does not": B. F. Skinner, cited in A. Bandura, *Social Learning Theory* (Englewood Cliffs, N.J.: Prentice-Hall, 1977), p. 203.

233   This is what: Jean-Paul Sartre, *Being and Nothingness*. Trans. by H. Barnes. (New York: Philosophical Library, 1956), p. 633.

Chapter 12

PAGE

268   In fact, Freud: Sigmund Freud, "Formulation on the Two Principles of Mental Functioning." *Standard Edition*. (London: Hogarth Press, 1961), pp. 12, 213–226.

273   "From the first": Betty Friedan, *The Feminine Mystique* (New York: W. W. Norton, 1963).

277   "We must surrender": Chogyam Trungpa, *Cutting through Spiritual Materialism* (London: Shambhala, 1973), p. 25.

278   "illusory circle of fire": Alan Watts, *The Way of Zen* (New York: Vintage, 1957), p. 47.

Bibliography

Allen, Woody. *Side Effects*. New York: Ballantine, 1975.

Assagioli, Roberto. *Psychosynthesis: A Manual of Principles and Techniques*. New York: Hobbs, Doorman, & Co., 1965.

Beckett, Samuel. *Waiting for Godot*. New York: Grove Press, 1954.

Berne, Eric, M.D. *Games People Play*. New York: Grove Press, 1967.

Chodorow, Nancy. *The Reproduction of Mothering*. Berkeley: University of California Press, 1978.

Diagnostic and Statistical Manual of Mental Disorders III, American Psychiatric Association, February 1980.

Dinnerstein, Dorothy. *The Mermaid and the Minotaur*. New York: Harper & Row, 1976.

Ellis, Albert, and Robert A. Harper. *A New Guide to Rational Living*. Hollywood: Wilshire Book Co., 1975.

Ekman, Paul, and Wallace V. Friesen. *Unmasking the Face*. Englewood Cliffs: Prentice-Hall, Inc., 1975.

Erikson, Erik. *Childhood and Society*. New York: W. W. Norton, 1963.

Fagan, Joen, and Irma Lee Shepherd. *Gestalt Therapy Now*. New York: Harper & Row, 1970.

Feldenkrais, Moshe. *Awareness Through Movement*. New York: Harper & Row, 1972.

Ferrucci, Piero. *What We May Be*. Los Angeles: J. P. Tarcher, Inc., 1982.

Freud, Sigmund. "Formulation on the Two Principles of Mental Functioning." *Standard Edition.* London: Hogarth Press, 1961.

————. *A General Introduction to Psychoanalysis.* Translated by Joan Riviere. New York: Washington Square Press, 1952.

————. *Civilization and Its Discontents.* Translated by James Strachey. New York: W. W. Norton & Co., 1961.

Friedan, Betty. *The Feminine Mystique.* New York: W. W. Norton, 1974.

Fromm, Erich. *The Art of Loving.* New York: Bantam, 1956.

Haley, Jay. *Problem Solving Therapy.* San Francisco: Jossey-Bass, 1976.

Herrick, Neal. "How Dissatisfied is the American Worker?" *Society,* January/February 1981.

Hinsie, Leland E., and R. J. Campbell. *Psychiatric Dictionary.* 4th edition. New York: Oxford University Press, 1977.

Holmes, T. H., and R. H. Rahe. "The Social Readjustment Rating Scale." *Journal of Psychosomatic Research,* No. 11, 1967.

Horn, Jack. "Smaller Is Better," *Psychology Today.* June, 1978, p. 24.

Jones, Landon Y. *Great Expectations.* New York: Ballantine, 1980.

Kazantzakis, Nikos. *Zorba the Greek.* Translated by Gerald Wildman. New York: Simon and Schuster, 1952.

Keen, Sam. *What to Do When You're Bored and Blue.* n.p.: Wyden Books, 1980.

Kelly, James. "Unemployment on the Rise." *Time,* February 8, 1982, pp. 22–29.

Kierkegaard, Soren. *Either/Or.* Translated by David F. Swenson and Lillian Marvin Swenson. Garden City, N.Y.: Doubleday, 1959.

Kopp, Sheldon. *An End to Innocence.* New York: Bantam, 1978.

Kubler-Ross, Elisabeth. *On Death and Dying.* New York: Macmillan, 1969.

Lasch, Christopher. *The Culture of Narcissism.* New York: Warner Books, 1979.

Lo Picolo, Joseph, and Leslie Lo Picolo, editors. *Handbook of Sex Therapy.* New York: Plenum Press, 1978.

Lowen, Alexander. *Bioenergetics.* New York: Coward, McCann & Geoghegan, 1975.

————. *The Language of the Body.* New York: Collier, 1971.

McLuhan, Marshall. *Understanding Media.* New York: McGraw-Hill, 1964.

————. *The Medium Is the Message.* New York: Bantam, 1967.

Maloney, Lawrence D., and John J. McCann. "Middle Age, the Best of Times," *U.S. News and World Report.* October 25, 1982, p. 67.

May, Rollo. *The Courage to Create*. New York: Bantam, 1976.

————. *Love and Will*. New York: Dell, 1974.

Miller, Arthur. *Death of a Salesman*. New York: Penguin, 1976.

Morgenthau, Hans, and E. Persons. "The Roots of Narcissism," *Partisan Review*, XLV:3, 1978.

"Newsline." *Psychology Today*. April 1982.

Ornstein, Robert E., editor. *The Nature of Human Consciousness*. San Francisco: W. H. Freeman, 1973.

"The Other Half: Partners in Pain." *American Health* (May-June, 1982), p. 44.

Pelletier, Kenneth. *Mind as Healer, Mind as Slayer*. New York: Delta, 1977.

Piaget, Jean. *The Construction of Reality in the Child*. New York: Basic Books, 1954.

————, and Barbel Inhelder. *The Psychology of the Child*. New York: Basic Books, 1969.

"Poll Results: On the Job." *Saturday Review*. May 1980.

Reich, Wilhelm. *Character Analysis*. Translated by Vincent R. Carfagno. New York: Simon and Schuster, 1972.

————. *The Mass Psychology of Fascism*. Translated by Vincent R. Carfagno. New York: Farrar, Straus, & Giroux, 1970.

Reik, Theodore. *Masochism in Sex and Society*. New York: Pyramid, 1976.

Schumer, Fran R. "Downward Mobility," *New York Magazine*, August 16, 1982, p. 23.

Shapiro, David. *Neurotic Styles*. New York: Basic Books, 1965.

Sheehy, Gail. *Passages*. New York: Bantam, 1977.

Sheler, Jeffery L. "Why So Many Workers Lie Down on the Job." *U.S. News and World Report*, April 6, 1981.

Trungpa, Chogyam. *Cutting through Spiritual Materialism*. Boulder and London: Shambhala, 1973.

U. S. Bureau of the Census. "Current Population Reports," Series P-20,#349, and earlier reports.

U. S. National Center for Health Statistics. "Vital Statistics of the United States," 1978, annual.

Watts, Alan. *The Way of Zen*. New York: Vintage, 1957.

————. *Psychotherapy East and West*. New York: Ballantine, 1969.

"Why Some People Can't Love." Linda Wolfe interview with Otto Kernberg. *Psychology Today*. June 1978.

Yankelovich, Daniel. *New Rules*. New York: Random House, 1981.

ABOUT THE AUTHOR

Dr. David Brandt is a clinical psychologist in practice in San Francisco. He teaches at the California School of Professional Psychology and has been a lecturer for the Department of Psychiatry, University of California Medical School. Dr. Brandt and his wife, Laurie, a psychotherapist, live by the ocean north of San Francisco, California.